From Backpack to Briefcase

From Backpack to Briefcase

Mastering Etiquette for Career and Personal Success

Leanne Pepper

Rock's Mills Press
Oakville, Ontario
2017

Published by
ROCK'S MILLS PRESS
All rights reserved. Published by arrangement with the author.

Copyright © 2017 by Leanne Pepper.

Photo credits: Cover, © Can Stock Photo/jana3000; Page 28, from top, © Can Stock Photo/photography 33, © Can Stock Photo/hfng, © Can Stock Photo/sjenner13; Page 34, from top, Matthew Henry/flickr, David Stover; Page 37, © Can Stock Photo/aurielaki; Page 43, from top, © Can Stock Photo/iofilolo, © Can Stock Photo/dolgachov; Page 47, both photos, David Stover; Page 87, courtesy the author.

For information, including Library & Archives Canada CIP data, please contact the publisher at:
customer service@rocksmillspress.com.

Dedication

Throughout my life one person has always been there during those difficult and trying times: I would like to dedicate this book, and everything I do, to my brother Randy Pepper.

In addition to Randy, I have been surrounded with strong supportive women: my mom, Peggy Pepper, and my sisters-in-law MaryAnn and Carlyle Jansen, and Helen Kennedy.

I am grateful to my stepson, Travis Belanger, for being my first student, and for helping me to market this book. I am so proud of Travis, who now has his own marketing business, MKTG-101.

Thank you to Michelle Stone for assisting with the children's etiquette classes, and thank you to my nephews Nazrik and Willem Jansen for willingly attending my etiquette boot camps.

I would not be the person I am today without the love and support of my husband Tim Belanger ... thank you, Tim!

Contents

Introduction ... 1

1. Personal Presentation ... 3
- DRESS TO IMPRESS ... 4
- PUT YOUR BEST FOOT FORWARD ... 7
- YOUR PERSONAL PRESENTATION CHECKLISTS ... 11

2. How to Work a Room ... 14
- MAKING YOUR ENTRANCE ... 14
- THE HANDSHAKE ... 15
- INTRODUCTIONS ... 18
- BODY LANGUAGE ... 21
- WORKING THE ROOM ... 22
- THE ART OF GOOD CONVERSATION ... 24
- CONCLUDING YOUR CONVERSATION ... 27
- CONCLUSION ... 30

3. How to Dine Like a Diplomat ... 31
- THE BASICS ... 31
- ORIENTING YOURSELF ... 35
- THE COURSES ... 39
- CHOPSTICKS ... 50
- EATING OUT ... 52
- DINING IN SOMEONE'S HOME ... 53
- WHAT TO DO IF ... 55
- MAKE IT A HABIT ... 57

4. At the Office ... 58

THE BASICS ... 58

MEETINGS ... 60

HOW TO DELIVER A SPEECH ... 65

VISITING AN OFFICE ... 67

MAKING AND TAKING TELEPHONE CALLS ... 68

EMAIL ETIQUETTE ... 73

TEXTING TIPS ... 76

CUSTOMER SERVICE SKILLS ... 76

Conclusion ... 79

ACKNOWLEDGEMENTS ... 81

INDEX OF KEY TOPICS AND TIPS ... 83

ENDORSEMENTS ... 85

Checklists

What You Should Wear and What You Should Not Wear to an Interview, Meeting or Networking event ... 6

Pre-Interview Checklist ... 11

Dos and Don'ts of being a Great Listener ... 24

Dos and Don'ts at the Dinner Table ... 49

Photographs

Exchanging Business Cards ... 28

Orienting Yourself at the Dinner Table ... 34

Holding a Wine Glass Properly ... 34

The Formal Place Setting ... 37

Holding a Soup Spoon Properly ... 43

Holding a Knife and Fork Properly ... 43

Knife and Fork in Resting Position ... 47

Knife and Fork in Finished Position ... 47

Introduction

Table manners are what typically come to mind when we hear the word "etiquette." Many believe that the whole business is irrelevant to them, so long as they stay away from posh places and people. But the reality is you cannot afford to ignore etiquette – not if you want to land a good job, network effectively, solidify strong business partnerships, secure a raise, or be awarded a promotion.

Hundreds of recent graduates and young professionals I have worked with over the past several years can testify to the powerful effects of well-cultivated social graces. One of the most memorable of these testimonies occurred in December 2015. As the general manager of the University of Toronto's Faculty Club, I had been preparing for our annual holiday buffet. Lunch service was just beginning when a young gentleman approached me in the main lounge, smiling warmly with his hand extended to shake mine. After introducing himself, Chirag said: "Ms. Pepper, I have to thank you. I took your etiquette course a couple of years ago. Because of your guidance, I landed the most amazing job: I am now the youngest professor at Northeastern University."

Chirag went on to explain that the recruitment process had involved not only a standard job interview, but also a reception and formal dinner. He told me that he had been able to fall back on what he had learned during my etiquette seminars in order to make the best impression possible during these networking opportunities. After offering him the position, his new employers confided in Chirag that they had been hesitant to hire him at first, given how young he was. Only after interacting with him during the reception and dinner did they know that he was the perfect person for the job: they had been able to witness firsthand how mature, respectful, and professional he was. In fact, Chirag recalls his new employers explicitly said they chose him because of his refined social graces.

Less than six months later, Chirag got in touch with me again to share even more impressive news. By then, he had received three other offers of employment. He began his latest position as an assistant professor of Engineering at the University of Toronto that same summer.

I have told you this success story to illustrate that etiquette is not some posh business, concerned only with frivolities like remembering to say please and thank you. Rather, etiquette is about putting the people around you at ease, making them feel comfortable in your presence, and assuring them that you can be relied upon to behave professionally and respectfully in any setting. As Chirag's experience demonstrates, the ability to project calm confidence in high-pressure circumstances can open up fantastic, even life-changing, opportunities.

In this book, you will learn the skills and strategies that Chirag used to land his dream job. These same skills and strategies will help you master networking events, job interviews, meetings with potential business partners, dinners with clients, and negotiations with your colleagues and superiors. The sooner you begin to master the art of good etiquette, the sooner you can expect success in your professional life.

ONE
Personal Presentation

Imagine arriving at a job interview, a meeting with a potential business partner, or a networking event where you will be introduced to some influential individuals for the very first time. The impression you make on these important people will stay with them for a long time, influencing your prospects of working for or collaborating with them. Because you never get a second chance at making that crucial first impression, it's important to get it just right.

The tricky part is, first impressions are often made before you even shake hands with or introduce yourself to someone. The moment you walk into a conference room, restaurant, banquet hall, or office, others are (consciously or unconsciously) taking note of the way you have decided to present yourself: your attire, grooming, posture, facial expression, demeanor, and so on. They do this for good reason, as they want to ensure the individual they decide to hire or collaborate with possesses several key features. First, they are seeking professionalism: a potential employer, for example, wants to be confident you will represent his or her business in a respectable way. Second, they want to work with someone who remains calm under pressure (and an important networking event or job interview is the perfect place to test your stress management skills). Third, they are looking for someone who projects confidence – a trait typically conveyed through good posture and a collected demeanor.

In short, your personal appearance speaks volumes. That means you need to do some prep work in order to make the most of that moment when you meet your future employer or business partner for the very first time. In this chapter, you will learn how to present yourself in a way that projects the professionalism, confidence, and capability that these important people are looking for. Following the grooming, attire, and self-presentation recommendations outlined below will prepare you to make a strong first impression in any professional setting – from networking events to interviews – and to maintain that good impression after you have landed your dream job.

DRESS TO IMPRESS

A carefully chosen outfit is one of the simplest ways to create the aura of professionalism employers want to see. Arriving at an interview in appropriately professional attire sends two messages to your potential employer. First, you are demonstrating that you care enough about your interview and your potential future with the company to have invested time and energy in your appearance. Second, you are showing that you are aware of the professional appearance that will be expected of you, should you be offered the position. So, clothing can be a quick and effective way to signal both your professionalism and investment in a position, allowing your interviewer to move beyond a consideration of your appearance, and focus instead on your skills, education, and accomplishments.

The general rule of thumb is that your outfit should be appropriate for a person filling the role for which you are applying. Rather than opting for clothing that reflects the position you currently hold – say, a student or entry-level worker – dress with your next position in mind. Wearing jeans, sneakers, and other lecture hall-appropriate garb to a job interview reminds your potential employer that you are fresh out of school, and therefore inexperienced in and unaccustomed to the work world. Instead, show your interviewer just how mature and professional you are by dressing the part.

So how do you determine what kind of outfit is suitable for the workplace you are applying for? First, do your research. Some organizations expect their employees to don suits every day, while others follow a "business-casual" dress code. You'll also have some broader clues based on your field. For example, law firms typically have more formal dress codes than tech start-ups: you would want to wear a suit for an interview at the former, but perhaps khakis and a button-down shirt to an interview for the latter. If in doubt, it is always best to err on the side of formality: a professional outfit that ends up being slightly too formal for the workplace you are applying to will go over better than an outfit that falls below their standards. Going too casual can imply that you do not value the opportunity being presented to you, or that you did not care enough about the interview to put some time into preparing yourself.

Second, opt for safe, classic pieces over flashy ones. For those applying to work in more formal settings, suits should be navy or charcoal, with a white shirt, black shoes, black belt, and leather briefcase or computer case. Choose socks that match the colour of your pants (which means you should never be wearing white socks!). Women should wear stockings that are neutral in colour, or that match their skirts or pants. Patterned stockings should be avoided. The same rules apply when interviewing for a position at an organization with a business-casual dress code: safe choices include khaki pants or a skirt, white shirts, black or brown shoes, a black or brown belt, and a leather or nylon briefcase or computer case. These simple colours are almost universally well received: because they are not distracted by the loud pattern of your shirt or the wild colour of your shoes, your interviewer will be able to focus on the valuable contributions you can make to their company. By contrast, bright colours and intense patterns may not only distract from what you have to say; they can also be interpreted as flashy, obnoxious, and tasteless.

Third, ensure that whatever pieces you've opted to wear fit properly, and are clean and pressed on the day of your interview. Suits should be professionally tailored. Casual pants for both men and women should be altered so they do not drag along or pool on the floor. Shirts should not be so large that they cannot be tucked into your pants without bunching up. Women must be cautious to avoid skirts that are too tight or too short. If you find yourself repeatedly tugging a skirt or dress down, it is likely both too tight and too short. Generally, no more than one hand's length of your thigh should be exposed when you are sitting with both feet flat on the floor. Similarly, avoid low-cut blouses: no more than one hand's length of your upper chest should be exposed. Wearing clothes that fit well will not only create a professional image; they will also let you focus on performing your best in your interview, rather than on constantly adjusting your outfit out of discomfort. Conversely, stained and otherwise unclean clothing is hugely distracting for your interviewer, and will detract from what you are saying.

Fourth and finally, remember to top your outfit off with appropriate accessories. As mentioned above, briefcases or computer cases should be in dark, neutral tones. Be careful to keep both the inside and out clean and tidy: when you open them, others will get a glimpse of what is within. These cases carry your work, so one that is messy and disorganized can imply to a potential employer or partner that you treat your work with similar disregard. Women should coordinate their briefcases with their handbags, choosing the same or complementary colours for both. Dark leather handbags are the best, most classic choice, and as with your outfit as a whole, your handbag should not have any flashy features such as spangles, jewels, tassels, sparkles, and so on. The same rules apply to your belt: studs and metallic designs are inappropriate. Opt instead for leather that matches your outfit, and keep it between one-half and three-quarters of an inch in width. For women, jewellery should be kept to a minimum: a few classic pieces, such as stud earrings, at most. Keep your shoe choice similarly simple: black is always the best choice. Running shoes, hiking boots, clogs, tall leather boots, sandals, open toed shoes, and platform heels are inappropriate. Women should also be careful to avoid heels that are too high: anything over two inches is unprofessional. And, as with the rest of your outfit, be sure to keep your shoes clean and polished.

To summarize, consider this checklist of what you should and should not wear to a job interview, business meeting, or networking event:

Do:	Don't:
✓ Select an outfit appropriate for someone filling the position you are applying for.	☒ Select an outfit that is overly casual, or implies you are only recently out of school.

✓	Buy pieces in classic colours and cuts.	✗	Wear brightly coloured, boldly patterned pieces.
✓	Keep your outfit clean and pressed.	✗	Wear excessive, flashy, large pieces of jewellery.
✓	Keep your shoes clean, polished, and free of scuff marks.	✗	Opt for sandals, clogs, tall leather boots, platform heels, hiking boots, open-toed shoes, sneakers, or high heels over two inches.
✓	Tailor your suit and otherwise ensure your clothes fit well.	✗	Wear very short, tight skirts, or low-cut, transparent blouses
✓	Pick neutral stockings, or ones that match your pants or skirt.	✗	Pick heavily patterned or brightly coloured stockings.
✓	Match your socks to the colour of your pants.	✗	Wear white socks.
✓	Opt for a dark leather, classic handbag.	✗	Carry a handbag with spangles, sparkles, jewels, or tassels.
✓	Coordinate the colour of your handbag and briefcase (e.g., dark leather).	✗	Allow your briefcase to become messy, dirty, or disorganized.
✓	Wear a leather belt between one-half and three-quarters of an inch in width that matches your outfit.	✗	Wear a metallic belt, or one with studs and other adornments.

PUT YOUR BEST FOOT FORWARD

Picking the perfect outfit is just one piece of the puzzle. To make a stellar first impression, you must ensure you are well groomed and presenting yourself in the most professional way possible. By taking the simple steps outlined below, you will arrive at your interview feeling confident and able to let your achievements remain the focus.

1. Be aware of your scent. Strong body odours are often immediately noticeable and will distract the person you are meeting with from what you have to say. Shower daily, and find a mildly or non-scented deodorant that works for you.

It is equally important to avoid colognes, perfumes, body sprays, and other scents that may be overly strong. Always remember that your future employer or business partner could have a sensitivity or allergy to scented products, and the last thing you want to do during your interview or meeting is make them feel uncomfortable or unable to focus.

2. *Maintain an oral hygiene regime.* Bad breath is just as unpleasant as body odour. Brush, floss, and rinse with mouthwash twice daily, and see your dentist on a regular basis. When you are in the office or another environment where you expect to run into others regularly, brush your teeth after every meal – this will ensure your breath stays fresh, and your teeth, free of food. Before entering an interview or meeting, use mouthwash or a mint. Avoid gum, however: you want to avoid constant chewing and other loud mouth sounds as you are speaking and listening.

3. *Care for your skin.* Your potential employer or business partner will spend the majority of your meeting looking at your face. Make an effort to keep blemishes under control by washing and lightly moisturizing your face twice daily. If you experience more serious acne, see a dermatologist to learn how to best care for your skin.

4. *Put extra effort into your hands.* Much like your face, your hands are always visible, and will be your first and only point of physical contact with your potential employer when you shake hands. Ensure they are clean and well cared for! Avoid biting your nails or cuticles, as this will leave them ragged and unsightly. Conversely, avoid growing your nails excessively: they should be no longer than half-an-inch. A good rule of thumb is that if you cannot pick up a dime, your nails are too long and need to be trimmed. Men and women alike should invest in a professional manicure, especially immediately before an interview, business meeting, or networking event. Opt for clear polish over bright colours, patterns, or designs, all of which may be interpreted as signs of immaturity or unprofessionalism.

5. *Avoid or conceal body adornments.* Some people have very strong opinions about piercings and tattoos, so you do not want to risk offending or putting off a potential employer or business partner by prominently displaying any you may

have. Pick clothing that conceals your tattoos, such as shirts with full-length sleeves if you have tattoos on your lower arms, or long pants if you have any on your ankles. Remove any visible piercings.

Beyond these five basic rules, there are a few other things to which men and women must pay particular attention.

For Men:

Pay special attention to your hair. Invest in a good cut, and have it trimmed on a regular basis – roughly once every two months, depending on its length. When going for an interview or business meeting, ensure you have washed your hair and combed it into place. In sum, you want to avoid leaving your hair to appear unruly or unkempt.

The same rules apply to body hair: if you have facial hair, keep it well groomed by trimming regularly. Remember to check your facial hair for crumbs before entering a networking event, interview, or meeting. Even if you have facial hair, your neck and upper chest should be shaved to below your T-shirt line. If you are clean-shaven, make a special effort to avoid developing a five-o'clock shadow: shave daily, and a second time in the evening if you have a later appointment. Finally, be sure to groom your eyebrows, nostrils, and ears: regularly remove any stragglers to maintain a clean, well-kept appearance.

For Women:

Your hair also requires special attention. Regardless of its length, ensure that it is clean and tidily styled. If you have longer hair, it should be pulled back while you are in professional settings, for two reasons. First, keeping your hair out of your eyes and off your face creates a more professional, poised look than loose, flowing styles. Second, keeping your hair pulled back guarantees that you will not touch or fiddle with it during your meeting – these are common responses to nervousness that are distracting for your interviewer, and make you look anxious and lacking in confidence. To ensure a professional appearance, try a sleek ponytail or a bun.

Just as with hairstyles, make-up can be used to create a

professional impression. A good rule to abide by is that your make-up should enhance your natural features; it should not be readily noticeable or distracting. Remember that you want your interviewer to be able to focus on your education, skills, and accomplishments – not your neon eyeliner. To this end, opt for a natural colour palette, and avoid metallic, sparkly, or brightly coloured liners, mascaras, eye shadows, and lipsticks.

To draw attention to your eyes, sparingly apply brown or black mascara, and a very thin brown or black liner, if any at all. Pick a neutral-toned eye shadow, such as light brown, taupe, or beige, depending on your skin tone, to enhance the shape of your eyes. Make-up can also be used to improve the appearance of your skin, but be careful to avoid using foundations that are too light or too dark for your skin tone, or layering it on too thickly; you want to avoid the appearance of a line where your foundation ends and the uncovered skin of your neck begins. Instead, invest in a high-quality foundation or tinted moisturizer that blends into your skin perfectly. Spend time consulting with a professional to find your ideal match. Powder can be sparingly applied to absorb oil, helping keep you from appearing clammy and nervous.

Lastly, apply a muted lipstick, gloss, or, at the very least, lip moisturizer. You want to wear something on your lips, since nerves can often cause them to become dry, chapped, and otherwise uncomfortable and distracting. Be careful, however, to pick a type of lip-wear that does not smear, or transfer onto your teeth easily. This is especially important if you will be eating or drinking during your meeting: bright lipstick stains all over your glass, cutlery, and napkin are far from pleasant. Your best bet is to avoid overly bright, bold colours. For example, while red or pink lip colours are often acceptable in professional settings, purple, orange, black, and the like are not. Soft pinks, reds, and other muted tones that match the natural colour of your lips are always safe options that will keep your lips from looking dry. Professional consultants in most make-up stores can help you pick a shade and consistency that works well for you. In sum, strive for a natural look with your make-up that will allow you to feel comfortable, and will not be distracting for the person you are meeting with.

YOUR PERSONAL PRESENTATION CHECKLISTS
In this chapter, you have learned the dos and don'ts of personal presentation: what you should strive to obtain – and what you should avoid – when preparing yourself to attend a job interview, business meeting, or networking event. Picking a professional outfit and taking time to groom yourself appropriately are extraordinarily simple, straightforward steps, but the pay-off for taking them can be huge. Never underestimate the power of a strong first impression: just as you take the time to pull together a portfolio of your work, research the company you are applying for, or practice answering interview questions, you must also take the time to cultivate your appearance. If you look the part, you will be able to devote your undivided attention to explaining what you have to offer your potential employer or business partner in the way of education, skills, and experience, rather than being distracted by an uncomfortable, ill-fitted outfit you constantly have to adjust, or by the glances your interviewer is stealing at your unpolished shoes.

To make it easy for you to feel confident and well prepared on interview day, I have prepared two "cheat sheets" you will find below. These are quick reference guides you should consult before heading to your interview or meeting. (You may even find it convenient to photocopy the list so you can have it at hand while you prepare.) Being able to check off each of these points will put you at ease with regards to your self-presentation, so you can stop worrying about how you look and focus instead on selling yourself to your future employer or business partner.

A Pre-Interview Check List for Men
Before you leave the house:
✓ Have you showered, applied deodorant, and brushed your teeth?
✓ Are your hands clean, and your nails trimmed?
✓ Is your hair washed and combed?
✓ Are you clean-shaven, or is your facial hair neatly

trimmed? Are your eyebrows, ears, nostrils, and chest hair well groomed?
- ✓ Have you chosen an outfit that projects professionalism, and is appropriate for the workplace you are applying for?
- ✓ Are your pants and shirt clean and pressed?
- ✓ Do your socks match the colour of your pants?
- ✓ Does your belt match your outfit?
- ✓ Is your briefcase or laptop bag clean and well organized?
- ✓ Are your shoes clean, polished, and free of scuff marks?
- ✓ Have you removed any piercings and covered your tattoos?

Before you enter your interview or meeting:
- ✓ Have you checked your teeth for food, and used mouthwash or a mint? Have you removed any gum you may have been chewing?
- ✓ Are your hands clean and otherwise well prepared for that first handshake?
- ✓ Have you checked your facial hair for crumbs?
- ✓ Is your hair still combed neatly?
- ✓ Are all of your buttons and zippers done up?
- ✓ If you are wearing one, is your tie straight?

A Pre-Interview Check List for Women

Before you leave the house:
- ✓ Have you showered, applied deodorant, and brushed your teeth?
- ✓ Are your hands clean, and your nails trimmed?
- ✓ Is your hair cleaned and neatly styled? Is it pulled back off your face and out of your eyes?
- ✓ Have you chosen an outfit that projects professionalism, and is appropriate for the workplace you are applying for?
- ✓ Is your outfit clean and pressed?
- ✓ Do your socks or stockings match the colour of your pants or skirt?
- ✓ If you have opted for a belt, does it match your outfit? Is it between one-half and three-quarters of an inch?
- ✓ Is your briefcase or laptop bag clean and well-organized? Does it match your handbag?

- ✓ Are your shoes clean, polished, and free of scuff marks? Is your heel lower than two inches?
- ✓ Are you wearing minimal, classic jewellery?
- ✓ Have you removed any piercings and covered your tattoos?

Before you enter your interview or meeting:
- ✓ Have you checked your teeth for food, and used mouthwash or a mint? Have you removed any gum you may have been chewing?
- ✓ Are your hands clean and otherwise well prepared for that first handshake?
- ✓ Are all of your buttons and zippers done up?
- ✓ Have you applied some form of lip make-up? Did you check your teeth for lipstick?
- ✓ Has your eye-make up smudged?
- ✓ Have you sparingly applied powder to your face, to avoid appearing clammy?
- ✓ Is your hair still neatly styled, out of your eyes, and off of your face?

TWO
HOW TO WORK A ROOM

Once you have carefully cultivated your personal appearance, the work of making a strong first impression has only just begun. Now that your potential employer, business partner, or professional contact has visually sized you up and determined, based on your attire and grooming, that you appear professional, they will be waiting for you to confirm their initial judgments with your words and demeanour. What you say and how you say it will demonstrate that your professionalism and confidence are not merely superficial: your conversation skills will prove that you are well-equipped to represent your future employer's company or your business partner's organization.

In this chapter, you will learn how to enter an event, the dos and don'ts of shaking hands, topics to avoid discussing in professional settings, and how to listen well. Whether you're at a business dinner, job interview, or networking event, these skill sets will ensure you are making everyone around you feel comfortable. In turn, the individuals you are looking to impress will be able to focus on your skills and credentials, rather than being distracted by your poor posture or inappropriate questions.

MAKING YOUR ENTRANCE
Recall from the last chapter all of the preparatory work that goes into making you look professional before you even leave home. All that work gets noticed when you first arrive at a networking event, business meeting, or job interview. The entrance you make is critically important for establishing a strong first impression.

One of the easiest ways to sabotage your own entrance is poor timing. Showing up to an interview or networking event late implies that you do not care about it or the people hosting it. It will also feel easier for you to walk into a room with only a few people inside, as opposed to dozens or even hundreds of people who have already been conversing for some time. Finally, arriving early will allow you to step into the washroom for a few minutes before making your entrance; use the extra time to run through your checklist from Chapter 1!

At a networking event or business function, people's eyes tend to gravitate towards the entrance to the room. Being aware of this fact allows you to use it to your advantage. Before you walk through the doors, take a deep breath and ensure you are standing up straight, practicing good posture. Then, walk calmly and confidently into the room, and step to one side of the entrance. (You want to avoid standing in the doorway, so you are not preventing others from coming and going.) Pause briefly to make yourself visible to those who are already at the event, and to survey the room: try to spot key individuals you were hoping to meet and speak with. Do not head immediately to the bar or the food; instead, circulate through the room to make your presence known to the key people there. Every time you meet someone new, shake his or her hand.

THE HANDSHAKE

Although the gesture is best known as accompanying introductions, there are other circumstances in which you should shake someone's hand. These include when:
- you are ending a conversation and parting ways with someone;
- you are renewing an acquaintance, or formally greeting someone you have met before;
- someone enters your office, cubicle, or home;
- you are leaving a business or social event. Handshakes are a means of respectfully saying goodbye.

Moreover, there are also circumstances in which it is inappropriate to shake hands, or the gesture should be avoided. For example, you should not shake hands if:
- the person you are greeting is holding something. Instead, politely acknowledge that you would usually offer a handshake, but can see that his or her hands are full.
- you are sick. Your new contact will be unpleased to find out that you have a cold *after* he or she has touched your hand. Rather than offering a handshake, explain that

you want to avoid passing your cold along.
- the person you are greeting is physically unable to shake your hand (for example, if he or she has had a stroke, or is older). Instead, place your right hand over your heart, make a slight bow, and say "It is a pleasure to meet you."

In certain social circumstances, handshakes have to be negotiated uniquely. For example, in European countries, the savvy man lets the woman offer her hand first. In other countries, however, women are not to shake hands with men at all. If you will be travelling for an interview or business meeting, be sure to do your research before you arrive.

Remember from the last chapter that your hands will be your only point of physical contact with your potential employer, business partner, or new professional contact, so they must be clean and well cared for. Handshakes are particularly unpleasant when they are clammy or wet. To avoid a slippery shake, carry tissues or antibacterial wipes with you, and use them discretely in the washroom before your interview, or before and during your networking event. Some unscented antiperspirants may also help reduce sweating from your palms, but be sure to experiment with these well in advance of a meeting or event to ensure you are not offering a hand that feels slimy. Also avoid wearing large rings that might interfere with your handshake or hurt the person you are meeting. Finally, in the winter, remove your gloves when you arrive at an interview, meeting, or networking event; handshakes should involve direct palm-to-palm contact.

If you are at an event where there will be food and drinks, you also need to be careful to ensure your hands are *available* for shaking! There are two ways to avoid being caught off guard. First, make introductions easier by avoiding the food and drinks table. If your hands are full of hors d'oeuvres, you will have to awkwardly juggle your plate to free up a hand to shake with. Worse still, you risk having unclean, sticky fingers when a new acquaintance offers his or her hand. Avoid these unflattering circumstances by carrying your glass or plate in your left hand, leaving your right free (and clean!) for shaking. Try having a snack or light meal before leaving home, so that you only have a few bites to eat at your event, rather than standing next to the buffet.

Second, be the one to initiate the handshake. As soon as you are being introduced or are introducing yourself to someone new, do not hold back: extend your hand immediately, with a warm smile. Your actions will be interpreted as confident and direct, signalling your ability to take initiative, and your eagerness to forge a professional connection. That said, taking the initiative should be restricted to handshakes exclusively: gestures of affection, by contrast, should be avoided, as they risk being misunderstood. Similarly, overly casual gestures, like "fist bumps," will indicate your immaturity and lack of professionalism.

Now that you have extended your hand for the shake, make sure to follow through with stellar execution. Follow these steps for a handshake that projects confidence:

1. Establish eye contact, and maintain it throughout the entire handshake. However, be careful not to intimidatingly stare your new contact down. Steady eye contact should be complemented with a warm smile.
2. Stand up when being introduced to someone. Do not shake someone's hand while they stand and you sit. (There are a few exceptions to this rule: for example, in circumstances where it would be awkward to stand, you do not have to.)
3. Position yourself appropriately. Standing too far away implies you are keeping your distance, perhaps out of dislike, while standing too close can make your new contact feel uncomfortable. So, just before you are about to shake hands, take a carefully calculated step towards the other person, ensuring you are close enough to comfortably clasp hands with a slightly bent elbow.
4. Establish web-to-web contact, with the palms of your hands fully secured against each other, rather than merely touching fingers. Your grip should be moderately firm: neither limp-wristed, nor bone-crushing.
5. After establishing contact, pump your clasped hands twice, smoothly and firmly. These pumps should be initiated from the elbow, rather than the shoulder.
6. Do not forget to actually introduce yourself! As you are shaking hands, say your full name, first and last. More

details on verbal introductions follow below.

Lastly, there are a few things you should avoid doing while shaking hands. Do not:

1. Shake hands overly aggressively, or crush your new contact's hand in your grip. Some people attempt to demonstrate their dominance by flipping the other person's hand over so that it is palm up. This gesture will come across as rude and excessive. Instead, keep your palms facing each other, with your thumbs directed towards the ceiling.
2. Rush the shake. Take the time to fully grasp and pump hands, rather than placing your hand in the other person's only to immediately retract it. Too quick a handshake can imply that you do not value meeting this new person, and would rather rush off elsewhere.
3. Linger in the handshake position. Once you have pumped your hands twice, let go. If you continue to hold hands with your new contact, it may be perceived as inappropriate, overly affectionate, and awkward.
4. Refuse to shake someone's outstretched hand. When someone extends his or her hand to you, accept the shake! Declining will be seen as rude.
5. Shake with a limp, lifeless hand. As you will be reminded below, the handshake is one of the most important forms of body language, and people read our body language as indicative of our personalities. A limp handshake implies you lack confidence, are unable to hold your ground, and will be easily convinced to do as others say. Project self-assuredness with a firm handshake.

INTRODUCTIONS

You will need to use your perfected handshake when introducing yourself to others. Introductions need to be made in the following situations:
- ✓ When you recognize someone;
- ✓ When you arrive at a gathering where you do not know some of the other attendees;
- ✓ When you have been seated next to someone you have never met before;
- ✓ When you are meeting a friend of a friend.

As with handshakes, there are slightly different protocols for introductions in different countries. For example, you may be expected to introduce yourself in some places, while in others it is polite to wait to be introduced. Again, do your research before arriving and be sensitive to the different expectations maintained in different cultures.

When introducing yourself, be sure to state both your first and last name. Do not, however, give yourself an honorific such as Mr., Ms., Doctor, Professor, and so on. Referring to yourself using these terms will be interpreted as rude and conceited. By contrast, however, you must indeed use an honorific when introducing someone else. Never assume that you may call someone by his or her first name; only after they give you permission or invite you to call them by first name may you do so. In the meantime, use an appropriate honorific such as Mr. or Ms. If the individual you are introducing has a title, such as doctor or professor, use that instead of Mr. or Ms.

You must also be conscious of those you are introducing. Always state the name of the person who is senior in rank first. For example, when introducing an executive to an assistant, you would state the name of the former first: "Mr. [executive's name], I'd like to introduce Mr. [assistant's name]." When introducing a client to someone working within your organization, make an effort to make the client feel like the most important person. To that end, state his or her name first: "Mr. [client's name], I'd like to introduce our director, Mr. [director's name]." After introductions have been made and an event or meeting unfolds, it is important that you can remember the names of your new contacts. Name badges or tags are typically provided at networking events for this precise purpose. When provided with a blank name badge at the start of an event, write your name clearly and in large letters, so people will be able to read it easily. A tag written in tiny print will render you less approachable, since no one wants to put themselves in the embarrassing, awkward situation of having to squint at your badge. After preparing your name tag, avoid your first instinct to swing your right hand across your chest and stick it to your left lapel. Instead, position the badge several inches below your right shoulder and smooth it out firmly so that it will stay securely in place.

The location of your name badge is so crucially important because it will help your new contacts remember your name, and vice versa. When you extend your right hand for a handshake, your line of sight will be naturally guided to the other person's right shoulder, where his or her name badge should be placed. Both of you will accordingly be able to see and learn each other's names as you make your introductions. This is why it is important to avoid placing your name badge in other, less typical areas, such as on your purse or laptop bag: you will force the people you are meeting to search for your badge, and will in turn break eye contact, weakening the impression you make upon them.

To maximize the effectiveness of your name badge, carefully select an outfit that lets it stand out. Keep the right shoulder area of your shirt or jacket free by placing corsages, broaches, and decorative pins on the left side of your lapel. Similarly, take the time to select an outfit that a name badge will stick to well. You want the badge to stay firmly in place and remain straight, so opt for fabrics that will prevent it from drooping or peeling off. Finally, women should ensure that the cut of their top allows for a name tag to be placed relatively close to the right shoulder: tags that are placed too low may inappropriately draw attention to the chest.

Similar rules apply when you are presented with a name tag that hangs from a lanyard. Adjust the lanyard length so that the tag hangs straight, and not too low; you want to make it easy for your new contact to quickly read your name. If you are wearing a collared shirt, neatly tuck the cord beneath your collar. Again, women should avoid hanging their tags in a way that draws attention to the chest. Men and women alike should opt for outfits that allow a lanyard to hang straight and avoid snagging or going askew.

Sometimes, name badges and tags are not provided, at which point you must make an extra effort to retain the names of the people you meet. Remembering someone's name is one of the simplest ways to make a good impression, as it suggests you genuinely cared about your meeting and found this individual interesting. There are three strategies you can use to help you remember names, the combination of which is known as the IRA formula. First, associate their name with your initial **impression** of them: take note of their appearance, height, how they speak, or if they look similar to someone else you know. Take stock of these visual details as you listen to your new contact say his or her name, and you will be better able to associate the name with a face. Be careful, however, not to base your impression of someone too deeply upon their clothing, since they will not be wearing the same thing the next time you meet. Second, your memory of a name will improve the more times you **repeat** it. As you speak with your new contact, insert his or her name into your dialogue. For example, if you were just introduced to Heather, part of the ensuing conversation you might have with her could be: "So Heather, what do you do for work? How long have you been in that business? What did you go to school for, Heather?" Actually saying your new contact's name will ensure you recall it in relation to the discussion you had together. Finally, **associate** the person's name with unique details about him or her. For example, if Heather has an uncommon job, or comes from a city you have always wanted to visit, you would mentally hook her name to that special thing about her. This last strategy has the added benefit of helping you remember something important about the new people you meet, in addition to their names.

BODY LANGUAGE

Like attire and grooming, posture speaks volumes. It can either be your downfall, by conveying defensiveness or shyness, or it can reinforce your professionalism and confidence. Always be sure you are standing or sitting erect, with your shoulders gently pulled back and down. Slouching and otherwise poor posture makes you look tired, dishevelled, and lazy. Your chin should be positioned neutrally or levelly: push it up too high and you are signalling arrogance, but keep it pulled back too low, and you are making yourself appear timid and reserved. To obtain the perfect positioning, be conscious of your eye line: you want to be able to comfortably look directly in front of you, into the face of the person you are speaking with. You do not want to be glaring down your nose at him or her, nor do you want to be sheepishly glancing upwards.

Your posture should convey your openness to meeting new people and participating in discussions. To that end, keep your arms and legs uncrossed. Crossed arms make you appear defensive or even hostile, and discourage people from approaching you. Crossing your legs is particularly problematic if you are seated at a crowded table, since it crowds the sitting space of those next to you. Rather than risking kicking the person seated beside you, keep both feet flat on the floor. Moreover, crossed legs and other positions that expose the bottoms of your feet are interpreted as offensive or distasteful in some cultures. Strive to make everyone around you feel comfortable by avoiding this position. Here are a few other postures and gestures to avoid, to ensure your body language sends the right message:

- Do not clench your hands into fists, as they will make you seem nervous and tense.
- For the same reason, do not grip your hands, arms, or wrists.
- Avoid cracking your knuckles.
- Keep your hands out of your pockets.
- Do not play with your hair or clothes. You will distract others from your conversation, and appear nervous and jittery.
- Avoid making others feel uncomfortable by standing too close to them. Acquaintances and professional contacts should maintain apprtoximately four feet between each other when interacting.
- Try to reduce any nervous fidgeting. Keeping relatively still, while appearing natural, projects a calm and collected appearance, whereas pacing, wringing your hands, tapping your feet, and so on conveys stress.

WORKING THE ROOM

Once you have made your stellar entrance, it is important to circulate throughout the room at the perfect pace. You want to ensure you have the opportunity to meet and speak with as many people as possible, while simultaneously avoiding offending anyone by appearing flighty.

Always remember that the purpose of attending a networking event is to meet new people and forge connections with them; if you spend the entire time alone, or conversing with people you already know, there is little point in attending at all. Do not be a wallflower: avoid standing or sitting near the outer walls of the room, where you will surely become more of an onlooker rather than a participant in conversations. Instead, gravitate towards the center of the room, as this is where the most important people will be, and where it is harder to be left out of discussions. Welcome others to introduce themselves or insert themselves in a conversation you are already having by making eye contact and smiling warmly. People will not be inclined to speak with you if you look frosty and unwelcoming.

While you do want to make new connections, be careful to avoid sabotaging a potential relationship by intruding upon conversations. If two people are visibly deep in conversation, it is not a good time to approach them. Interrupting their dialogue may make you appear rude or overly aggressive, and such a negative first impression is worse than no impression at all. For similar reasons, avoid these behaviours when you are at a networking event:

- Do not engage with your phone. Turn it off and leave it in your coat or purse. If you are constantly looking at it, texting, or calling others, you will appear preoccupied and as though you have priorities other than being present at the event and conversing with the people who are actually there.
- Do not table-hop. Circulating an event and meeting new people is indeed your goal, but you do not want to appear flighty or over-eager. Spend enough time with each new contact to engage in a substantial conversation before moving on to the next. No one will remember you if you merely introduce yourself and then leave!
- At the same time, however, do not spend the entire event talking with just one person. If others see you deep in conversation with the same individual for a prolonged period of time, they will be less likely to approach you and introduce themselves.

☒ Avoid drinking alcohol. You want to make the best first impression possible, and alcohol will reduce your inhibitions, making you more likely to do or say things you otherwise would not.

THE ART OF GOOD CONVERSATION

While working the room, you want to ensure that you captivate all the new people you meet by engaging them in rewarding conversations. The easiest way to maintain stimulating dialogue is to prepare yourself. Read up on the people you expect to meet, the companies they work for, and their latest accomplishments. Also be prepared to intelligently and respectfully comment on any recent happenings in the news, arts, and culture. This is especially important if you are travelling to a different country: your new contacts will be impressed if you have taken an interest in their culture and are able to engage in discussions about it.

Being well prepared is also important for your role as a listener. Listening well is just as (if not more!) important than speaking well when you are in a networking environment, for two reasons. First, people want to feel as though they are respected and valued, and when they can tell you are listening intently to what they have to say, you will make them experience those positive feelings. Second, your ears will never get you into trouble. Sometimes, things we say can be interpreted as offensive or inappropriate, but attentive listening will never convey the wrong message.

The table below provides some "dos and don'ts" to help you become a great listener.

Do:	Don't:
Maintain eye contact to signal that you are engaged and paying attention.	Be overly enthusiastic in your efforts to convey engagement.
Keep an open mind, and respect the other person's opinions.	Be excessively critical of or openly judgmental about the other person's comments.
Be alert and actively try to digest the information you are hearing.	Take notes on the other person's thoughts in front of him or her.

Eliminate distractions (make sure your phone is turned off, and that you are not trying to eat, drink, or otherwise multi-task).	Answer or look at your phone or participate in another activity while the other person is speaking.
Make a genuine effort to give the person who is speaking your undivided attention.	Interrupt and begin speaking yourself.
React to the speaker in appropriate ways through your facial expression and comments.	Become emotionally "deaf" by staring blankly or failing to react.

Of course, participating in a conversation means you will also have to speak yourself at some point. Make sure that your end of the conversation does *not* feature any of these negative aspects:

- ☒ Small talk and gossip;
- ☒ Going on about yourself in great detail;
- ☒ Correcting another person's vocabulary or grammar, or pointing out his or her mistakes;
- ☒ Your personal likes and dislikes;
- ☒ Sex, politics, religion, and any other controversial topics that are likely to inflame emotions;
- ☒ Money or salaries;
- ☒ Complaints or negative comments that may be interpreted as whining;
- ☒ Bad-mouthing your company or an individual you do not like;
- ☒ Trashing the competition;
- ☒ Your clients' confidential information;
- ☒ Confidential company information, including sales figures, pricing, or information about products that are about to be launched;
- ☒ Customer complaints;
- ☒ When speaking to people for whom English is not the first language, do not ask "Do you understand me?"

By contrast, there are plenty of topics that are appropriate for professional conversation. The best way to initiate a dialogue that your new contact will enjoy is to ask polite, respectful, positive questions that focus the conversation on him or her. To draw more information out of an individual, try asking open-ended questions beginning with "what" and "how," as you will be more likely to get responses that are longer than a single word and that allow the conversation to flow.

For example, try asking some of the following questions:
- ✓ How do you know the host?
- ✓ What neighbourhood do you live in?
- ✓ How long have you lived there?
- ✓ What do you do for work?
- ✓ How did you get into the business?
- ✓ What do you enjoy about your profession?
- ✓ Do you travel often?
- ✓ What are your hobbies?
- ✓ What are your long-term goals?

In sum, you want to ask short, respectful questions that will help others open up to you. Be careful, however, to avoid bombarding your new contact with questions: ask only a single question at a time, and listen thoroughly to the response. Instead of immediately ploughing on and asking yet another question, thoughtfully respond to what the other person has said. In other words, use questions to jump-start a conversation, and then allow the dialogue to take its natural course. Having a good sense of humour, a positive attitude, and an open mind will go a long way in facilitating that natural progression.

Similar rules apply when you are participating in conversations with more than one other person. Make an effort to keep everyone in the group involved in the conversation, rather than focusing all of your attention on a single individual. In group settings, you will also impress others if you know how to step in and fill embarrassing voids in the conversation. Silences can be awkward, and knowing how to break them in appropriate ways will make others appreciate your presence. Lastly, learn when to discuss business and when not to. Often, you can take cues from others to know whether a given circle is most comfortable conversing about work, or if they would prefer more casual conversation.

CONCLUDING YOUR CONVERSATION

When your conversation has come to an end, and you are either moving on to meet someone else or leaving a networking event altogether, you may exchange business cards with your new contact. Save this exchange for the conclusion of your discussion, once you feel you have started to build a relationship with the person you have just met. Opening a dialogue by whipping out your card and saying "give me a call" may seem rude – as though your priority is to give your contact information to as many people as possible, rather than to establish genuine connections with a select few. Instead, when your conversation is wrapping up, ask for permission to provide your new contact with your card: say, "Would you mind if I gave you my card?" If you have just met someone very senior who is clearly in a position of authority over you, he or she should be the one to initiate the exchange of cards.

Remember, your business card represents you and your company. It should therefore convey an appropriate corporate image using professional language. Your card should also clearly explain your position or role – after all, it will (you hope) be used by your new contact to get in touch with you following an interview, meeting, or networking event. You want the people to whom you give it to be able to recall who you are and what you do.

Be sure to keep a sizeable stock of your cards on hand whenever you attend an interview, business meeting, or especially a networking event. Print your cards on high-quality paper, and carry them in a professional cardholder to keep them crisp and clean. Presenting a dirty, crumpled, and otherwise poorly cared for business card is worse than not presenting one at all: it signals that you fail to invest time and effort in the work that that business card represents.

When preparing to offer your card, never lick your finger in an effort to get one loose. Simply slide a card out from its holder, and present it using your right hand, with the type facing upwards. When you receive someone else's business card, study it closely and comment on it before putting it away. Do not put it in your back or hip pocket, as this is an insult in some countries. Instead, gently place the card in-

The exchange of business cards is an important part of networking events and other meetings. In North America it is done relatively informally (left) but in Asian cultures the exchange is more formal, with cards being presented and received with both hands (bottom).

side your jacket pocket. Never write on someone else's card.

When traveling abroad, have the text of your card translated into the appropriate language. Keep one side as it was, in English, and print the other side in the language of your host country. Just as with your standard cards, these dual-language cards should always be carried in a case. Present the card with the side written in the host language facing up. I prefer presenting my business card with both hands. Take particular care with your business cards if you are travelling to Japan, where they are exchanged with great ceremony. There, business cards are a means by which to convey status and hierarchy. Your card must therefore include your title, so that your rank can be easily determined. In Japan, cards are presented with two hands, a slight bow, and a nod. When receiving a card, be sure to receive it with two hands and to read and study it with extra attention, as the entire exchange process carries great weight. To repeat, if you place the card in your hip or back pocket, or in your wallet which you then place in your hip or back pocket, your gesture will be seen as offensive. Instead, place the card into your jacket pocket close to your heart.

Once you have concluded your conversation and exchanged cards with an important new contact, you might take a moment in private to document what you discussed. Slip away to the washroom or another quiet spot and jot down some notes about the person and what you talked about together. Never do this in front of your new contact, however, as it might appear that you are not paying close enough attention to absorb what he or she is saying. Your privately recorded notes will help you recall particularly important conversations with individuals you would like to follow up with, as the details of what was discussed with which person are easily forgotten after events where you will be meeting dozens of new people. Use your notes to follow up with your new contacts the following day: within 24 hours of the event, send each a personal, hand-written thank-you message. In that message, be sure to mention something you discussed together the day before. For example, if your new contact mentioned that he or she was planning a vacation with his family, you might include something in your thank-you note along the lines of, "Have a great trip with your family." Referring to something you discussed will show your new contact you were listening as he spoke.

CONCLUSION

Networking is an art in itself. Stellar self-presentation, genuinely engaged listening, and the ability to hold a compelling conversation can make or break a business deal or employment contract. No matter how highly qualified, talented, or accomplished you are, established professionals will not be able to appreciate what you have to offer if you cannot communicate it in respectful, appropriate ways. In order to start or advance your career, you need to make a conscious effort to walk, talk, act, and dress like the professional you want to be.

THREE
How to Dine Like a Diplomat

I began this book by dismissing the myth that etiquette is merely about table manners. Indeed, in the past two chapters, I have explored the many aspects of professional interactions that involve making those around you feel comfortable and respected. While this chapter *is* about table manners, it is also about more than that: when you are conscious of your dining habits, and know how others will react to those habits, you will be able to put your dining companions at ease. In turn, you will all be able to focus on the engaging conversation you learned how to cultivate in the last chapter, rather than wondering which glass belongs to whom, or where to leave your soup spoon as you reach for the bread basket.

Knowing the dos and don'ts of the dinner table is crucial in today's job market, where so many interviews and business meetings are conducted during a meal. Plenty of my professional contacts who are well established in the business world have shared their "horror stories": recollections of the awkward, embarrassing behaviours they have observed while trying to conduct business over breakfast, lunch or dinner. Each of these stories invariably ends with lost business. What may seem like petty table manners could actually cost you a job, business deal, raise, or promotion. Meanwhile, the ability to project calm confidence while seated at the dinner table could open up a whole new world of professional opportunities.

THE BASICS
There are a few general rules you should follow regardless of whether you are dining in a restaurant, at someone's home, enjoying a formal dinner, or conducting business over breakfast. Before I delve into the details of place settings, how to hold your fork and knife, and how to eat the different courses in a standard meal, you must be familiar with these basic behaviours that will be expected of you throughout that meal. Keep these points in mind as the

foundation for your dining etiquette:

1. *Always follow your host.* When you arrive at the table, remain standing until (s)he invites you to sit, or until (s)he takes his or her own seat. If you are attending a cocktail party or another event where multiple people are expected, you may stand behind your chair until everyone has arrived. In addition to being polite and respectful, this will also provide you with a great opportunity to introduce yourself and meet the individuals with whom you will be dining.

Depending on the formality of the event, you may either seat yourself, or the gentlemen in your party may be expected to pull chairs out for the women. In the latter circumstance, the women are seated first, followed by the men. Always lift a chair gently off the ground when pulling it out or pushing it in to keep harsh scraping sounds to a minimum. To avoid a traffic jam, take your seat from the right: that is, as you are standing behind your chair, you will pull it out and sit down from your right-hand side. Similarly, if you need to excuse yourself at any point during the meal, you will stand and exit to your right.

The "follow your host" rule applies to every other step of the meal as well: before placing your napkin on your lap, taking your first sip of water, or beginning to eat, wait until your host makes the first move. Often, (s)he will say something to indicate that everyone else may begin to take these steps. For example, (s)he may say "Bon appétit," or raise his or her glass for a toast, signaling to everyone else at the table that the meal may commence.

2. *Maintain impeccable posture.* As I have explained in previous chapters, your posture speaks volumes. Signal your confidence and professionalism by sitting at the table with your spine elongated, chin level, and shoulders back. To maintain this posture and stay sitting up straight, you will need to bring your utensils up towards your mouth, rather than bringing your face down to the plate and slurping up your food.

Recall as well that your feet should always stay flat on the floor. Crossing your legs at the table merely increases your risk of kicking the people seated next to or across from you. Worse still, you will also remember from the last chapter that showing others the soles of your feet can be deeply offensive to some. Our shoes are always in contact with the ground, so directing your foot towards someone else by crossing your legs may be taken as suggesting that you equate him or her with dirt. You do not want to risk implying to your dining companions that you lack respect for them.

Finally, your hands should be resting on the tabletop at all times: do not place them in your lap. Avoid projecting tension or aggression by clenching anything – utensils, your water glass – with a tight fist. Your elbows should never make it onto the table. Keep them down by your sides; avoid allowing them to ride up as you attempt to cut your food. Practice this posture privately by eating a meal on your own with paper plates tucked under each arm. Trying to keep the plates in place will ensure you keep your elbows low.

3. Keep pace with everyone else. Make an effort to eat at roughly the same rate as your dining companions. In particular, if anyone excuses herself, or takes a break from eating, put your knife and fork down. Conversely, do not eat painfully slowly, so that you are the last one left with food on your plate long after everyone else has finished. You should move through each course at the same pace as everyone else, so that no one feels rushed, or as though the meal is dragging. Keeping pace with each other in this way will ensure the meal unfolds at a smooth, consistent rate and will in turn allow everyone at the table to eat comfortably.

4. Take small bites. Putting only a small amount of food on your fork reduces the likelihood that it will slip off and into your lap as you move your fork to your mouth. Large bites, by contrast, are more difficult to chew and swallow quietly, with a closed mouth. They also take longer to finish, and you do not want to get stuck having just taken a massive bite of food right when someone asks you a question! (See the "What To Do If…" section below for pointers on how to manage this scenario.)

5. Put your phone away. Your phone should be switched off and left in your bag or coat throughout any meal. Never put it on the table or in your lap, and never answer it while you are supposed to be conversing with your dining compan-

Hold your wine glass by the stem between your thumb, forefinger and middle finger and allow the rest of your fingers to rest naturally on the base (including your little finger! Do not keep your pinky pointed outward).

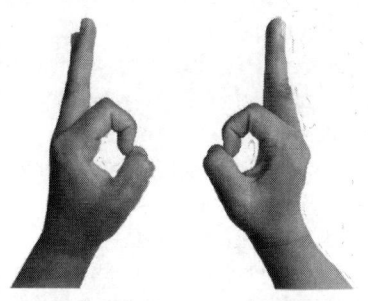

If you touch your index fingers to your thumbs while keeping the rest of your fingers together, your left hand will look like a "b" and your right, a "d." You can use this symbol in private to practice orienting yourself to a formal place setting: your left hand, which forms the b, will hover over your bread and butter dish, to the left of your main plate, while your right hand, which forms the d, will be closest your drink, on the right of your main plate.

ions. Using your phone during a dinner party is just as rude as looking at the clock repeatedly: it gives the impression that you have better things to do, or other places you would rather be.

If you are expecting a crucial call that you simply cannot miss, let your host know in advance. Inform him or her that you believe you will be receiving an important call and may have to step away, and be sure to apologize in advance. If you do indeed receive the call during the meal, excuse yourself and take the call outside – never at the table.

ORIENTING YOURSELF

Once you have followed your host's lead and taken your seat at the table, you will notice the variety of plates, utensils, and glasses laid out for you. Although the precise setup may vary slightly, it is fairly consistent across most restaurants (and even in most homes).

The Napkin

Again, following your host, you will begin by positioning your napkin. Take it from the table and unfold it while it is by your side, under the table. Leave it folded in half, and place it in your lap, with the crease facing your waist. Never tuck the napkin into your shirt collar.

Once you begin eating, you may use the napkin to ensure your face and hands remain clean and free of crumbs. If you feel there is some food on your face, wrap your napkin around your index finger and delicately dab it at the corner of your mouth. To remove food from your fingertips, discreetly wipe them on the inside of your folded napkin while keeping it in your lap. This ensures that when you place your napkin on the table at the end of the meal, it will not be covered in fingerprints.

Indeed, this is one part of the way in which you will signal you have finished eating: in addition to placing your utensils in a particular way, which I outline below, you will place your napkin on the table at the end of your meal. After wiping your fingers and mouth for a final time, pinch your napkin in the centre of the fold and place it neatly on the tabletop. Do not bunch or ball it up.

Place Settings

There are two tricks you can use to remember which plates and glasses belong to whom. First, think of BMW cars. For our purposes, BMW will stand for Bread, Meal, Water. This acronym maps on to your place setting, as your bread is to the left of your main plate, your meal will be served directly in front of you, and your water glass is just to the upper right of that main plate.

Second, if you touch your index fingers to your thumbs while keeping the rest of your fingers together, your left hand will look like a "b" and your right, a "d." You can use this symbol in private to practice orienting yourself to a formal place setting: your left hand, which forms the b, will hover over your bread and butter dish, to the left of your main plate, while your right hand, which forms the d, will be closest your drink, on the right of your main plate.

Use either of these two tricks to make sure you are drinking from the correct water glass, and placing your dinner roll on the correct bread plate. However, if the person seated next to you mistakenly claims your glass or plate, do not make a scene. Ideally, everyone else around the table will also adjust.

Utensils

Forks are always to the left of your main dish, while your knife and soup spoon are to the right. At the top of your plate are your dessert spoon and fork, as well as a spoon for your coffee or tea. I will detail the proper ways to hold and use each utensil below, in my discussion of the various courses in a typical formal meal.

Glassware

To repeat, your glass will be positioned to the upper right side of your main plate. Often, serving staff will fill each water glass individually. Occasionally, however, a pitcher will be provided for the table (this is most often the case if you are at a conference or seminar). If the pitcher has been placed in front of you, you are responsible for "serving" it. To do so, offer to fill the glasses of those seated next to you before filling your own.

The Formal Place Setting

1. Salad Fork
2. Fish Fork
3. Dinner Fork
4. Napkin
5. Butter Knife
6. Bread Plate
7. Dessert Spoon
8. Dessert Fork
9. Place Card
10. Salad Plate
11. Soup Bowl
12. Service Plate
13. Salad Knife
14. Meat Knife
15. Fish Knife
16. Soup Spoon
17. Tea Spoon
18. Seafood Fork
19. Water Goblet
20. Champagne Flute
21. Red Wine Glass
22. White Wine Glass
23. Sherry Glass

Formal Dinner Place Setting

This illustration shows the various elements that make up a formal place setting for dinner. Not every utensil or plate may always be present on every occasion.

Remember, do not take your first sip of water before your host does. When you pick up your water glass, hold it by the stem, rather than clutching it around the ball. This will keep the glass free of fingerprints. Keep your pinky tucked in as you take small sips of water throughout the meal. Gulping is not only loud and unsightly; it also increases the likelihood that you will wind up with ice in your mouth, which you will have to uncomfortably allow to melt in order to avoid crunching.

Generally, you should avoid drinking alcohol if you are at a job interview, business meeting, or networking event. However, if you do opt to drink beer, be sure to have it in a glass – do not drink it straight from the bottle. For wine, hold your glass by the stem between your thumb, forefinger and middle finger and allow the rest of your fingers to rest naturally on the base (including your little finger! Do not keep your pinky pointed outward). Just as with your water glass, this will eliminate unsightly fingerprints on the bowl. It will also keep your wine cooler for longer, as the warmth from your hands will not be in close contact with the wine. For these reasons, never cup your hand around the bottom of a stemmed wine glass. If you are presented with a stemless wineglass, hold it by its base.

If you are ordering a bottle of wine at a formal restaurant, the serving staff will present it to you upon delivering it to the table. Make sure you read the label and confirm that they have picked the correct bottle (for example, that they have brought the selection priced at $30, not a wine from the same vineyard priced at $300!).

The staff will then open the bottle and present the cork. If it is dry or smells "corky," the bottle may have gone off. Next, the staff will pour a small amount into your glass for you to sample. Swirl the wine gently, breathe it in, and take a small sip. You will be able to tell if the wine is not right, as it will taste tinny. If so, politely and graciously inform the staff that it is no longer good by saying something like, "I think this may have gone off…"

As you are drinking your wine throughout the meal, it *is* socially acceptable to swirl it in your glass. However, be careful to do this slowly and gently to avoid sloshing it over the side. When taking a sip, look into the glass, rather than over its rim.

THE COURSES
Different occasions, events, and venues call for different numbers and types of courses. In general, however, you will typically enjoy a soup, salad, main course, and dessert and coffee during a formal lunch or dinner, which may begin with a toast. In this section, I review how to go about eating each of these courses, including which utensil should be used for what, how to manoeuver particularly difficult pieces of food, and strategies to keep messes to an absolute minimum.

Toasting
Although not every meal will begin with a toast, your host may occasionally use one as a means to signal that everyone may begin eating. Most often, they are reserved for formal dinner parties. In this scenario, the host will offer the first toast. Do not overstep by trying to make the first toast yourself when you are in someone else's home. Simply raise your glass in response to your host raising theirs, and keep it raised as you listen to the toast. If you are at a small, informal dinner, everyone may remain seated as the toast is delivered. Conversely, if you are at a large, formal banquet, you may be expected to stand during a short toast, though not during a longer speech. The only time you *must* stand is when toasting to the Queen. When dining with large parties, it is customary to simply raise your glass, listen to the toast, and take a sip of your drink once it is completed. Members of smaller parties may touch their glasses to each other's. As you clink glasses with others, be sure to make eye contact, rather than looking at your drink. That said, remain conscious of your glass and to avoid spilling bring it very gently into contact with others'.

If you are the one hosting, you may wish to deliver a toast. First, make sure everyone's glass has been filled. It is not necessary, but you may wish to touch your fork lightly to your glass to get everyone's attention before you begin speaking. If you opt to do so, be very careful not to smash your stemware – be gentle! Once your party is listening, raise your glass and say something simple, such as: "It's a pleasure to have all of you here tonight. I have been looking forward to this night for a long time. Welcome." Never drink to yourself, or make the toast all about you; instead, it should serve to welcome your guests.

In some settings, your toast may need to be longer. In those cases, prepare your toast well in advance and rehearse it several times. Strive to be positive, witty, and interesting. Do not make any off-colour jokes. If you have been asked to deliver a longer toast but are not the person hosting the event, speak with the host in advance to ensure your content is appropriate and that no one will be embarrassed or uncomfortable. Throughout any toast, make eye contact with your guests or your host and smile warmly.

Bread and Dinner Rolls

Most often, a basket of bread will be provided for the table. If the basket has been placed in front of you, do not help yourself first. Instead, pick it up and offer it to the person to your left, asking, "Would you like a roll?" They should then return the basket to you, and you may take one roll before passing the basket to your right, after which it will circle the table counter-clockwise.

When it is your turn to pick a roll from the basket, choose the one on top, that is the most easily accessible. Do not dig through the basket, touching multiple rolls, before picking one, and do not break one in half, only to leave the second half in the basket. Lift one full roll from the basket and place it on the bread plate to your left. Never place your roll directly onto the table. As your roll is not a course of its own, do not move your bread plate in front of you; leave it in place to the left of your main plate. If you notice that the rolls being offered are particularly flaky, it is best to avoid them altogether: you will only get crumbs everywhere as you try to break pieces off.

Occasionally, a full loaf of bread will be served to the table. If a knife has been provided, and you are the one expected to cut the bread, use a napkin to hold the body of the loaf with your left hand, so you are not touching the loaf directly. Then, use your right hand to cut slices. If a knife has not been provided, you should still hold the body of the loaf with a napkin, break off a piece of bread with your other hand, and then take the piece you are touching with your bare hand.

As everyone around the table collects their rolls, the butter will also begin to circulate in the same way: if it is in front of you, offer it to the person on your left before serving yourself, and then pass it around the table counterclockwise. Take one dollop and place it on your bread plate in the five o'clock position. Your butter knife will rest on this plate parallel to the place setting, so keeping the butter in the five o'clock position will help you avoid placing the handle of your knife into it. If the butter is served in balls, take one full ball – do not slice one in half and leave the second half on the serving dish.

Use your butter knife – not the knife you will use for your main course – to butter your roll. Remember: this is a dinner roll, not a sandwich. Do not slice it open down the centre, butter it up, and take a bite. Instead, break off a small, bite-size piece, and butter just that bite. Always use your butter knife – do not mash your bread into the butter!

If you are offered olive oil in place of butter, pour a small amount into the five o'clock position on your bread plate, break off a small piece of your roll, and dab it lightly into the oil. Never pour oil onto the bread itself. To avoid drips, be sure to dip your roll only very lightly into the oil, and gently brush excess oil off on to your plate before lifting the piece of bread to your mouth.

Most importantly, take pains to avoid creating a mass (and mess!) of crumbs. Break your bread carefully and directly over your bread plate to keep any crumbs contained upon it. If, when your plates are cleared at the end of the meal, you notice bread crumbs beneath your plate, simply leave them. You never want to appear as though you are doing housekeeping by tidying up the table in any way. Never sweep your crumbs onto the floor or into your napkin. Instead, wait for a staff to bring a napkin or de-crumber and clean the table on your behalf.

Soup

The first course in a formal meal is typically the soup. Recall that your soup spoon is located on the far right of your plate, while the one above your plate is for dessert and coffee or tea. Hold your soup spoon in your dominant hand – the right, for most people – and rest it on your middle finger. Never clutch the handle by wrapping all five fingers around it.

Dip the spoon into your bowl to pick up a small mouthful: the spoon should be three-quarters full or less, so the soup does not slosh over the edge of the spoon and spill as you bring it up to your mouth. You may also prevent drips and spills by running the back of your spoon against the far side of your bowl before lifting it to your mouth, so that any excess on the bottom of the spoon slides back into the bowl.

Always scoop your soup using motions away from yourself, rather than towards. You can remember this using the saying, "Like ships that go out to sea, I spoon my soup away from me."

Begin by taking soup from the top and outer edges of the bowl, where it will be coolest. This way, you will avoid burning yourself or making an awkward, uncomfortable face after taking a mouthful of very hot soup. If the soup is steaming and clearly too hot to eat, do not blow on it; simply let it sit until it cools slightly.

Make an effort to eat your soup as quietly as possible. Never slurp it, or sip it from your spoon. This is also why your spoon should only ever be three quarters full: you want to be able to consume all of the soup that is on your spoon, so avoid taking too much. Similarly, keep your soup spoon quiet by dipping it gently into the bowl, rather than clanking it loudly. When your bowl is nearing empty, do not scrape your spoon along the bottom; instead, tilt it away from you, and gather your last spoonfuls where they are pooling at the far side of the bowl.

When you are taking a break from your soup, the spoon rests on the saucer below the bowl. Do not put your spoon on the tabletop, as you will stain the tablecloth. Also avoid leaving it in the bowl, as you will be more likely to accidentally hit it as you reach for your water or roll.

This photograph illustrates the proper way to hold a soup spoon. One should never clutch the handle of the spoon by wrapping all five fingers around it in a clenched fist.

This photograph illustrates the proper way of holding your knife and fork while dining.

When you have finished eating your soup, leave the bowl in place. Pushing it away from you will make it difficult for the serving staff to clear, while leaving it in front of and close to you will allow them to remove it without reaching too far over you.

Salad

A salad is often served before, after, or in place of soup. Most salads should be eaten using both your knife and salad fork: the one on the outside of your place setting, or furthest to your left. Usually, this will be the smallest fork, and a larger one will be located to its right for the main course. However, in some European settings, a salad is served *after* the main course, in which case your smaller salad fork will be located closer to the inside of your place setting, or to the right of the larger fork used for your main course. In either case, you will always eat the first course using the fork on the outside of your place setting, and work your way in.

In some restaurants, you may only be provided with a single knife and fork. In these circumstances, you might request a clean knife and fork from the serving staff after you have finished your salad, but you should always be conscious of the venue: in some restaurants, this will be entirely appropriate, but in others, it may come across as excessive, picky, or needy. Use your best judgment.

To eat your salad, hold your fork in your left hand and your knife in your right (reverse the two if you are left hand dominant). Practice holding and using your cutlery properly in private before a formal meal. Begin by opening your left palm and facing it towards the ceiling. Place the fork, tines up, in the palm of your hand on a slight diagonal, so the curved spot where the handle meets the tines is resting only on your index finger. Then, wrap your remaining fingers and thumb around the handle and turn your hand over, so the tines of the fork are facing down, towards the plate. Your index finger should still be resting lightly where the fork begins to curve. You will know you have the correct positioning if, when you look down at your left hand with the fork in it, you can barely see the handle of the fork, and you cannot see any of your fingernails except that of your index finger, which is pointing in the same direction as the fork.

Grasp your knife in the same way, but in your right hand: place it on a slight diagonal in your open right palm, so the section of the knife where the handle and blade meet is resting on your index finger. Wrap your three other fingers and thumb around the handle, and flip your hand over so the serrated edge faces down, towards your plate. Your index finger should be lightly resting on the top of the knife, on the flat, non-serrated side of the blade. Once you are comfortable holding your knife and fork in this way, you no longer need to gain the correct orientation by beginning with your palm facing up; this is only so you can practice grasping each utensil properly.

To eat your salad, use the knife to help push and anchor the leaves, vegetables, or fruit onto your fork. Both the tines of the fork and the serrated edge of the knife should always remain facing down, towards the plate. Do not flip the fork over and use it like a spoon. Instead, spear each piece of lettuce firmly so that you are able to bring the fork up towards your mouth while the tines remain down. Then, twist your wrist toward your mouth and slide the fork in.

That said, certain salads are notoriously difficult to eat. If you are choosing your own dishes – as opposed to enjoying a set menu – avoid ordering salads that will be difficult to manoeuver onto your fork. Salads with broccoli, blueberries, nuts, and other small pieces will invariably slide around your plate rather than spearing easily onto your fork (and they are also likely to end up stuck in your teeth!).

The best way to eat graciously and avoid making a mess is to take small bites. Take only a few leaves of lettuce onto your fork at a time, folding larger leaves in half so they fit in your mouth more easily, and slice larger pieces of vegetables into smaller bites. If absolutely necessary, you may turn the fork over, but use this as a very last resort; always try to order food that will be easy to eat while keeping your fork in the correct position.

When you would like to take a break from eating, rest your utensils on the plate – not on the table next to it. Place your knife on the plate with the end of the handle barely extending beyond the rim towards you, and the serrated edge facing inwards, or to the left, between the four and five o'clock positions. Place your fork over top of the knife, with the tines facing down, between eight and nine o'clock.

When you are finished your salad, your utensils maintain the same orientation, simply pushed together, so there is no space between them. The knife is on the right, with the handle on the rim of the plate, and the serrated edge facing in, towards the fork. The fork is on the left of the knife, also with its handle on the rim, and the tines facing down. Together, the knife and fork should be in the six o'clock position when you have finished eating.

Main Course

Most often, your main course will be served following the soup and/or salad. Ideally, your server will present the main dish in the 6 o'clock position, making it easiest for you to cut and eat. Never treat your plate like a steering wheel and "drive" it by spinning it around to a different orientation; even if your server has not presented it correctly, leave the plate as is and work with it as best you can.

If you are dining at a restaurant without a set menu, order a main course that is easy to eat. Never order lobster, shellfish, corn on the cob or other messy dishes during a formal business meeting or interview. Similarly, avoid ordering anything that you have never tried before, that you do not know how to eat, or that is the most expensive item on the menu.

To eat your main course, use the fork and knife that are remaining at your setting after your salad utensils have been cleared. Typically, the fork for your main course will be slightly larger than the one you used for your salad. Depending on the dish, the knife may be similar, or you may be presented with a larger, sharper knife if you have ordered something more difficult to cut, such as steak, for example.

Use your utensils just as you did to eat your salad: with the fork in your left hand and knife in your right, and the tines of the fork and blade of the knife facing down, towards your plate. If your dish requires little or no cutting – such as pasta, for example – use the knife to push and anchor each

How you position your utensils on your plate lets the server know whether you are simply taking a pause but plan to continue eating (top) or whether you have finished the course, in which case the server will feel free to clear your place.

bite onto the fork before lifting it to your mouth. If certain items on your dish must be cut – such as meat – use your fork to secure your food to the plate, and the knife to cut. To cut, simply bring the knife towards you; do not use it like a saw, or mash it into the plate. Remember, always keep your fork in your left hand with the tines facing down; do not flip it over and use it like a spoon, and do not transfer it into your right hand each time you take a bite.

Coffee and Dessert

For dessert, you will use the smaller fork and spoon usually placed above your main plate. Once the dish from your main meal has been cleared, move the fork down to the left and the spoon down to the right of the area where each course has been placed. Hold the fork in your left hand, just as you did during your main course or salad. The spoon goes in your right hand, resting on your middle finger, just as your soup spoon did. Use the spoon to slice small bites of soft desserts (such as a poached pear or tart), while you use the fork to hold the dessert in place on the plate. Eat each bite off of the spoon, not the fork.

Once again, be conscious of the type of dessert you are ordering. Avoid dishes that will be challenging to cut and eat tidily. Pieces coated in hard chocolate, for example, may be difficult to slice into bite-sized pieces. The last thing you want is to send food flying!

If you would like coffee or tea, you may move the cup and saucer down to the right of your place setting, to make it easier to add milk, cream, or sugar tidily. If sugar is offered in packets, and you do not use a full one, do not return the unused portion to the container. Instead, keep the remaining bit of sugar, fold the packet neatly in half, and place it on your saucer. After stirring any milk, cream, or sugar into your coffee or tea, return the spoon to your saucer. Avoid placing it directly on the table, as you will create a stain.

When drinking, loop your index finger through the handle of the cup, and allow the rest of your fingers to curl in – do not stick your little finger out. Lift only the cup to your mouth; leave the saucer on the table.

In sum, during each and every course of the meal, you

want to make your best effort to eat as quietly and tidily as possible.

Use the following checklist when you need a refresher on the dos and don'ts of the dinner table.

Do:	Don't:
✓ Follow your host: take his or her lead before starting any aspect of the meal.	✗ Help yourself before everyone has arrived.
✓ Bring your utensils up to your mouth.	✗ Bring your face down to the table.
✓ Have a snack before you arrive.	✗ Sniff your food hungrily.
✓ Use your cutlery gently and quietly.	✗ Loudly clank your cutlery.
✓ Avoid at all costs spilling your food and creating stains.	✗ Place your used cutlery onto the table.
✓ Take your time and eat carefully, with small bites, keeping pace with everyone.	✗ Finish your courses much more quickly or slowly than everyone else.
✓ Keep both hands on the table at all times.	✗ Leave your hands in your lap.
✓ Order simple dishes that are easy to eat and will not get stuck in your teeth.	✗ Pick your teeth at the table.
✓ Chew with your mouth closed.	✗ Speak with food in your mouth.
✓ Tuck your briefcase or purse under your chair, to keep it out of the serving staff's way.	✗ Hang your bag on the back of your chair or prop it up against your chair leg, where it will impede traffic.
✓ Excuse yourself if you need to cough, sneeze, or blow your nose.	✗ Apply lipstick, comb your hair, or otherwise groom yourself at the table.
✓ Try at least a little bit of everything on your plate.	✗ Ask for a doggie bag for your leftovers.

CHOPSTICKS

So far, I have focused on dining etiquette as it pertains to the West. However, if you will be visiting a restaurant that serves certain types of Asian cuisine, you must also be careful to avoid using your chopsticks in inappropriate ways. Stay away from these chopstick faux pas to avoid unintentionally offending any of your dining companions:

1. Vertical chopsticks (立て箸). At Japanese funerals, a bowl of rice is left with two chopsticks standing vertically in the center. You do not want to imitate this practice during your meal! When you place chopsticks straight upright in a bowl, it is said to bring bad luck. Instead, make use of the chopstick rests (箸置き) by your dish, or rest disposable chopsticks on the bag they came in.

2. Passing food (拾い箸). Another ritual at Japanese funerals is to pass bone fragments of the deceased from person to person with a pair of chopsticks. Again, avoid calling this practice to mind by picking up a piece of food with your chopsticks and passing it to someone else at your table. Often, it is best to just keep your food for yourself, and let others serve themselves from any shared dishes.

3. Placing chopsticks across a bowl (渡し箸). This is the equivalent of placing your knife and fork together in the six o'clock position: it indicates to the chef (and everyone around you) that you no longer want your dish. If you have not finished eating, then placing your chopsticks across your bowl can be interpreted as rude. Also avoid placing your chopsticks across each other while you are not using them. Instead, keep them straight and parallel, side-by-side. If you were not given any chopstick rests, place disposable chopsticks on the wrapper they came in. If your chopsticks are not disposable, place them along the left edge of your dish.

3. Talking with Your Hands ... and Chopsticks (踊り箸). If you are in the habit of gesturing with your hands as you speak, be sure to put your chopsticks down before you start chatting. Waving your chopsticks in the air, or using them to point at someone or something, is impolite and can get messy if there are any remaining bits of food on them.

4. Stabbing Food (指し箸). Do not use your chopsticks as spears. It is considered rude to stab your food with one or both chopsticks in an effort to pick it up. Also avoid using one of your chopsticks as a knife, to cut your food into pieces. Pretend the two chopsticks are attached, and always use them together in your dominant hand.

5. Sucking on Your Chopsticks (ねぶり箸). Just as you would not lick your fork or knife, never suck or chew on your chopsticks. Also avoid letting them dangle in your mouth while your hands are occupied, and never use your chopsticks to scratch your head (or any other part of your body).

6. Hovering over Food (迷い箸). Try not to let your chopsticks hover from dish to dish while you decide what to eat. Keep your chopsticks in their resting position while you weigh your options, and only pick them up when you know what you intend to grab.

7. Taking from Shared Dishes (逆さ箸). You are welcome to take food from shared dishes, but use the supplied utensils to do so. Some people turn their chopsticks around and use the thick side that has not been touching your lips to take food from a shared plate. Although this practice is well-known, it is impolite, since you are using the end of the chopsticks that have been touching your hands to dip into a shared plate of food. Instead, use extra chopsticks (取り箸) to transfer food from a communal plate to your own. When in doubt, watch to see what others do.

8. Moving Your Bowl (寄せ箸 ・ 持ち箸). Do not use your chopsticks to latch onto your bowl and pull it closer to you. Also avoid lifting a bowl with the hand that is holding your chopsticks (持ち箸). Instead, put your chopsticks down and use two hands to reach for a bowl and bring it closer to you.

9. Washing your chopsticks (洗い箸). Do not use a bowl of soup (or any other liquid at the dining table) to wash off your chopsticks. There is no need to "rinse" them.

10. Rubbing chopsticks together. Avoid rubbing wooden disposable chopsticks together. This is done to remove splinters from low-quality, inexpensive chopsticks, so doing this rudely suggests to your host that you think the chopsticks you have been given are of poor quality and inexpensive. Even if you are given disposable chopsticks, try not to do this unless they are splintery.

EATING OUT

There are some distinct differences between conducting an interview or business meeting in a restaurant and enjoying a meal in someone's home. First, you will most often have business meetings over breakfast, lunch, or high tea (usually between 3:30 p.m. and 5 p.m.). Dinner is usually reserved for special occasions, or for guests from out of town.

If you are the one responsible for organizing a lunchtime business meeting with a client, be sure to take the lead and schedule it confidently. Never ask your client where he or she wants to go. Instead, pick a restaurant that you know will be easy for your client to get to – not one that is most convenient for you. If you do not know your client, check with his or her assistant to see if he or she has any dietary preferences or restrictions. You do not want to bring a vegetarian to a steakhouse! Call the restaurant ahead of time to ensure they have availability on the day you would like to bring your client there, and make a reservation if possible. You do not want to waste your client's time by making him or her wait to get a table. When making the reservation, select the table: ensure it is far from the kitchen and washrooms.

When inviting your client to the meeting, be sure to make the call yourself – do not have someone else (like your assistant) call on your behalf. Clearly state the purpose of your invitation: have an agenda, and make it clear to your client why you would like to meet. The day before your scheduled meeting, confirm with your client the time and location.

Arrive early to your meeting to take care of all the details, such as coat check and parking, and to ensure the table you selected has been prepared. If possible, arrange with the serving staff to have the bill taken care of before your client arrives. It is your duty, as the one who arranged the meeting, to pay for the meal. Your client will take the best seat, so leave it vacant for him or her. Though you will be there early, do not start eating or drinking. When your client arrives, the table should look completely untouched. Allow him or her to order first, and follow their lead by ordering the same number of courses for yourself. Remember to avoid alcohol, and order dishes you will be able to eat easily, without making a mess, spilling, or getting food stuck in your teeth.

When you are treating a client to a business meal, you are filling the role of host. That means it is your duty to take charge and keep the meal moving along at an appropriate rate. If service is slow, or the meal is unsatisfactory, it is your job to say something. Never be rude or aggressive to the serving staff; instead, maintain a businesslike professionalism by speaking firmly, but politely.

Conversely, you may also be asked to meet with your manager or superior over a meal. Under those circumstances, be sure to arrive on time, appropriately dressed. The remaining rules still apply – i.e., you should avoid alcohol, order easy-to-eat dishes, and follow all the other etiquette pointers we have reviewed so far – with the exception that your superior will typically cover the bill. In this scenario, because you are not the one paying for the meal, do not order the most expensive thing on the menu, or things that you do not know how to eat (such as lobster, for example). Just in case, however, always bring your wallet with you. You never want to appear presumptuous by assuming that your meal will be taken care of.

DINING IN SOMEONE'S HOME

Colleagues and superiors may invite you to their home for dinner, often to celebrate a work-related success. When you are issued an invitation, respond as promptly as possible. Formal invitations will often include instructions regarding RSVPs; pay close attention to the details of these instructions, and always respond exactly as requested.

The rules for arriving at a dinner party are different than those regarding a networking event, business meeting, or job interview. Recall from the last chapter that you should be among the first to arrive at a networking event: you want to be there early to double-check your appearance and to avoid the stress of making an entrance in a packed room. By contrast, never arrive early to a dinner party at someone's home. Your host will invariably be running behind, struggling to put the finishing touches on the meal. So, you should actually arrive ten minutes *late*, to provide your host with a few extra minutes to prepare.

Never arrive empty-handed! Always bring a small gift to thank your host for having you. A bottle of wine is often a good choice, although you should always be confident that your host drinks alcohol – presenting a bottle of wine to a non-drinker would be inappropriate. Alternatively, you may bring a plant. Fresh-cut flowers are difficult and time-consuming for your host to handle: he or she must find a vase, fill it with water, trim the ends of the flowers, and so on, all while attempting to greet other guests and ensure the meal is on track. A potted plant, by contrast, can conveniently be left as-is.

When dining in someone's home, you will almost never be given a choice with regards to the menu. Typically, your host will ask each guest well in advance if they have any dietary preferences or restrictions. Often, you will be requested to provide this information in your RSVP. Beyond that, however, you will likely have little control over the food you are served. If there is something offered that you are not comfortable eating, do not question it or make a scene. Instead, simply try to eat around it. Your host should make an effort to serve foods that are relatively easy to eat, but if you are presented with something tricky, just do your best. Take comfort in the fact that everyone else will likely struggle too!

It is also important to do some research in order to determine how much you are expected to eat while in someone else's home. In some cultures, finishing absolutely everything on your plate indicates to your host that you are still hungry, so you will continue to receive plate after plate of food. In others, however, failing to finish your entire meal is considered rude, as it is thought to mean you did not enjoy or appreciate the food. So, be sure to investigate before you arrive. In almost all circumstances, you should at least *try* everything on your plate; avoid pushing things you do not like out of the way or refusing to try them entirely.

Always follow up with a thank-you note. Send your host a handwritten note in which you thank them for having you, and comment on the lovely meal. If someone has invited you to his or her home, it is respectful to reciprocate the invitation. If you cannot host – say, if your apartment is too small – invite them out to a restaurant for dinner instead.

WHAT TO DO IF...

Despite your best efforts, mistakes will occasionally happen at the dinner table. If you find yourself in a sticky situation, remember that the important thing is how graciously you are able to manage it and get the meal back on track. Below, I have compiled a list of less-than-desirable circumstances you might find yourself in, and what you should do to fix them (along with strategies for avoiding these situations in the first place).

If you get food stuck in your teeth: Avoid getting food stuck in your teeth altogether by ordering dishes that are easy to eat (i.e., no spaghetti)! If you order meat, ask for it to be cooked rare to medium rare, so that it is easier to cut and chew. Well-done meat will require greater effort to slice into small bites, and take longer to chew.

If, despite your best efforts, you feel that there is food in your teeth, never try to pick it out while seated at the table. Instead, excuse yourself and slip away to the washroom. When excusing yourself, remove your napkin from your lap before standing up, then drape it over the back of your chair. This will signify that you are not finished eating, and will be returning to your meal, whereas leaving your napkin on the table would indicate that you are done. Push your chair in before exiting the room.

If you notice food in someone else's teeth or on their face, graciously let them know. Never offer to remove food from someone else's face at the table.

If you must cough, sneeze, or blow your nose: Try your absolute best to avoid doing any of these things at the table. Instead, excuse yourself and slip away to the washroom. Remember to leave your napkin draped over your chair, not on the table, and push your chair in.

You may not have time to do all of this before sneezing. At the very least, you should turn away from the table and cover your mouth with your arm or napkin as you sneeze towards the floor. Never sneeze into the food or onto the person seated next to you.

If you drop something: You never want to appear as though

you are doing housekeeping. If you drop a piece of food or a utensil on the floor, do not pick it up or try to hide it by kicking it under the table. Let the staff come to your aid, and provide a new piece of cutlery or collect the dropped food.

If your order is incorrect: If the serving staff presents you with something other than what you ordered, never make a fuss. There are some circumstances in which you might want to request that your order be fixed. For example, if you are on a job interview, your potential employer might be interested to see whether you are confident and assertive enough to speak up. However, if you opt to ask the serving staff to fix the order, you should never be rude or obnoxious. Nor should you accept the order, only to badmouth the staff to your dining companion. Instead, gently and graciously inform the staff of the mistake and request to have it rectified by saying, "I believe I asked for…" or "I ordered _____, but I believe this is _____."

If you must speak with your server: Your server should stop by your table regularly to ensure you have everything you need. Avoid appearing needy or demanding by saving your requests for the next time they come by. However, if your server is not appearing regularly at your table, and you or your guest desperately need to speak with him or her, attract attention graciously and politely. Never snap your fingers or whistle. Instead, make eye contact, smile warmly, and nod to indicate that you need him or her to visit your table. When he or she approaches, always be respectful and kind, never berating or hostile.

If you are asked a question after taking a bite: Always be mindful when asking your dining companions questions. Avoid posing a question just as someone has taken a bite. Instead, do so when they have placed their utensils in the "resting" position. However, someone may ask you a question when you have food in your mouth. Never respond while your mouth is still full. Ideally, you will have taken a small enough bite to be able to chew and swallow relatively quickly. In the meantime, gesture to indicate that you have just taken a bite by placing a finger to your lips. Your companion will then give you time to chew.

MAKE IT A HABIT

Many of us do not adhere to the rules that govern formal dining, especially when we are enjoying a casual meal alone, or with friends and family. But these more relaxed, informal settings are actually ideal opportunities to practice everything you have learned in this chapter. If you treat every meal like a rehearsal for an important professional dinner, what may seem like foreign dining habits will eventually become second nature. When you do eventually need to execute perfect etiquette on a high-pressure occasion, like a job interview or business meeting, your dining skills will not only be impeccable, they will also come naturally. Being able to fall back on habitual table manners will allow you to focus your undivided attention on selling yourself to a potential employer, ensuring your client is comfortable, or negotiating the terms of a business deal.

It takes 21 days to begin to get into a pattern or routine. It takes 100 days for a new behaviour to become automatic. That means you have no time to lose! Start making dining etiquette a habit today by practicing at every meal.

FOUR
At the Office

Once you have landed your dream job or secured a promising business partnership, your work has only just begun. Collaborating with others in an office or other professional setting requires ongoing attention to etiquette: how you address, converse, and negotiate with your colleagues and clients will impact others' perception of you. It will therefore also impact your chances of being awarded a raise or promotion, of continuing business with your clients or partners, and of being offered new partnerships in the future.

In this chapter, you will learn how to behave with decorum and professionalism at work. This involves both small details that make a big difference – such as the way you enter someone's office – as well as higher pressure scenarios, like your ability to manage an effective, productive meeting. In addition to all of this new information, you must also remember the dos and don'ts of professional attire and grooming, handshakes, introductions, business card exchanges, networking, and dining that I have outlined in the preceding chapters. This should serve to reinforce the importance of habit-building: practice your table manners, professional dress, solid handshakes, and a respectful demeanor until they become second nature. That way, you will not have to think about this long checklist of workplace etiquette on top of your actual work!

THE BASICS
Certain rules apply no matter what company you work for, or whom you have established a business partnership with. Follow these rules of respect to ensure you develop strong relationships with your colleagues and clients, as well as a good reputation for yourself:

1. Respect the company's culture. This will entail living up to the social expectations others have of you as a newcomer to the organization – not trying to make those expectations change to match how you like to do things. For example, if you are expected to wear a suit and tie to work every day, you must do so. Do not show up in business casual attire. Refer to Chapter 1 to ensure your clothes are sending the message you want them to.

2. *Respect the company's hierarchy.* When you first begin working at a new organization, you will almost always have superiors working above you. Respect their rank and seniority by being polite and cordial at all times. Being disrespectful or dismissive of your superiors is a guaranteed way to develop a bad reputation among your colleagues, and become known for being difficult to work with. By contrast, you will be awarded more opportunities if your superiors enjoy being around and working with you.

3. *Respect your colleagues.* Be courteous to *everyone* you work with, no matter his or her role or status in the company hierarchy. Making enemies of anyone will do you no favours. It is particularly important to respect the privacy of your colleagues: if you are working in a shared office space, avoid eavesdropping on conversations, and avoid prying into others' personal affairs.

4. *Respect others' views.* Your clients, colleagues and superiors will undoubtedly voice personal views that you do not agree with at one point or another. Be respectful of their opinions. Remember that your ears will never get you into trouble, so it is always best to listen patiently and quietly rather than putting your own opinion forward as a "better" alternative. Everyone will admire your ability to handle disagreements gracefully. By contrast, no one wants to work with an argumentative know-it-all.

5. *Respect boundaries.* Work will be stressful at times, but you will be seen as professional and capable of managing high-pressure situations if you can stay calm, cool, and collected. Never cross professional boundaries and impose your worries on your coworkers or superiors – you want them to feel confident in your ability to manage crises. You should, of course, always ask for help when needed, but request guidance or assistance in a calm, polite way and never expect a colleague to put your deadlines above his or her own.

6. *Respect the company's equipment.* In shared workspaces, you all need to use the same equipment. Be respectful of ev-

eryone else's needs, and avoid hogging the copier, printer, computer, phones, and so on. Never use work equipment to meet your personal needs; the only thing worse than hogging the printer is hogging it to print off family vacation photos. If you borrow equipment, return it on time and in flawless condition.

7. *Respect everyone else's time.* Everyone is on a tight timeline, just like you. Be respectful of your clients', superiors' and colleagues' busy schedules by arriving on time to your desk in the morning, to meetings, and to other work functions. Also be sure to only take the designated amount of lunch or break time you have been allotted; you do not want to appear lazy or unmotivated by straggling back to your desk well after everyone else.

MEETINGS

Meetings are nothing more than an exercise in communication: you and your colleagues will be expected to speak to one another, listen to one another, discuss the various ideas proposed, and then decide upon one. In this way, meetings are a good way to facilitate effective communication between staff members and ensure that everyone feels his or her voice and opinion is heard.

To that end, it is important to speak in turn. Hopefully, the organizer of the meeting will have prepared an agenda. Follow it in order to ensure that everything that needs to be covered gets taken care of. For example, do not bring up point 5 on the agenda within the first few minutes of the meeting; this will disrupt the flow of the meeting and may result in points being missed.

Also ensure that you speak only when it is your turn. Specifically, you should wait for the organizer of the meeting to acknowledge you before delving into the point you would like to make. This is important because there are likely several other people waiting to speak as well. Starting to speak whenever you feel like it is disrespectful to everyone else who has been patiently waiting. Even if your comment is directly related to one that was just made, you still must wait your turn instead of bypassing someone else who has been waiting. If you think you will forget your comment, write it down. Then, when it is your turn, you can simply say, "I'd like to briefly return to the point about _____," and make your point.

If there is other business you feel must be attended to beyond what is listed in the agenda, do not just bring it up whenever you feel like it. Make an effort to review the agenda that is circulated well in advance of the meeting, and if you feel strongly that there is something additional that should be added, contact the organizer and request to have the addition made. Otherwise, the organizer will likely ask near the end of the meeting if anyone has any outstanding issues or other business they would like to address. At that point, you may bring up any related business that was not noted in the agenda.

To ensure the most productive meetings, participants must feel comfortable brainstorming and sharing their ideas. That means it is particularly important to remember point 4 from the list above during meetings, and be respectful of everyone else's views, even if they do not match your own. Never tear down someone else's idea and offer your own as a "better" alternative. One good strategy for managing differences in opinion is to ask for clarification or more information, rather than automatically and immediately dismissing someone else's idea. Voice your request in a cordial, welcoming manner by saying something like, "I'm not sure I understand. Can you give me an example?" Never be rude when questioning someone else, and avoid losing your temper at all costs.

If you have been invited to a meeting organized by someone else, there are a few rules you should adhere to in order to make your involvement as cordial as possible:

1. Well in advance of the meeting, review the minutes from previous related meetings. Knowing what has been discussed in the past will ensure you do not make a suggestion that has already been considered and dismissed. This preparation time will also give you an opportunity to start thinking in advance about solutions to problems you might like to pose during the meeting.

2. Arrive at the meeting room three to five minutes before the meeting is scheduled to start. This will give you

time to find a seat at the table, power up your computer, or take your notebook out. You do not want to be doing any such set-up when the organizer is attempting to begin the meeting, as it is distracting to others, and prevents you from devoting your full attention to what the organizer is discussing. Avoid at all costs having to enter a meeting that has already begun. Being on time demonstrates the respect you have for the team and their time.

3. As always, ensure your mobile phone is turned off, on silent, and put away in your bag or left at your desk. There is nothing ruder than taking a call, texting, or emailing while someone else is trying to share an idea. Even worse, having your phone ring loudly in the middle of a meeting will disrupt and distract everyone.

4. If the meeting is particularly long, the organizer may opt to schedule a break. Stick to the timelines provided and be sure you are back in the meeting room when you are scheduled to resume. Being late is disrespectful of everyone else's time, and suggests that you think you are more deserving of a longer break than those who made an effort to return to the table on time. You might also miss some important points if everyone opts to get started before you are back.

5. At the end of the meeting, stay for a couple of minutes to help the organizer tidy up the room. Throw out any left-behind garbage from coffee or food that has been provided, push chairs in beneath the table, and turn off the lights once everyone else has left.

6. Often, several "action items," or tasks you need to take care of, will arise during your meeting. Take careful notes regarding what you have been asked to do, especially if someone requests that you get in touch after the meeting to discuss something in greater detail. Be sure to follow up with everyone you promised you would follow up with!

If you are the one organizing a meeting, you need to take special care to ensure it goes smoothly. Your work begins well in advance of the actual meeting date. First, only call a meeting if you have actual business that needs to be attended to. Once you have determined what needs to be accomplished, figure out who should be present at your meeting in order to effectively discuss and manage the issue at hand.

Do not invite people to the meeting who have nothing to do with the issue; respect that they have other projects to work on and let them devote their time to those. By contrast, be sure that you invite all those who *are* involved with the issue you are hoping to discuss.

Send everyone a meeting invitation well in advance of the date you have selected. Not only will this ensure that people have time to prepare, it also increases the likelihood that their calendars will still be free. When picking a date, aim to make it as convenient as possible for the greatest number of people. That means avoiding Monday mornings and Friday afternoons. Also avoid scheduling meetings before or after office hours, which are typically between 9 a.m. and 5 p.m. For example, do not schedule a meeting at seven o'clock on a Monday morning or six o'clock on a Friday evening.

Make a similar effort to choose a location that is convenient for everyone and conducive to productive work. Ideally, you will have rooms designed to hold meetings in your office space, so that everyone can easily come together without having to devote travel time to get to the meeting. If that is not the case, and you must settle on an external location, avoid spots that are noisy and over-crowded, like rowdy bars or bustling coffee shops. Ideally, you want everyone to be able to sit around a table so they have space to use their laptops or notebooks. You also want everyone to be able to hear each other speaking, which is why calm, quiet spaces are ideal.

At least 48 hours before your meeting is scheduled to begin, you should circulate any minutes from previous, related meetings as well as your agenda for the coming meeting. This will give everyone a chance to get caught up if they were not present for previous meetings, or refresh their memory if they were. It will also give them the opportunity to ask to add any items to your agenda, if needed.

Before leaving home on the day of your meeting, remember to run through your checklist from Chapter 1. You want to appear put-together and professional, with the confidence and competence to run an efficient, productive meeting. Never arrive looking sloppy or haggard.

On the day of your meeting, arrive at the room you have

booked or meeting place you have settled upon at least 30 minutes early. If you are able, adjust the temperature of the room to ensure it is not too hot or too cold; you want everyone to be focused on the work at hand, not on their discomfort. Then, ensure the meeting place is clean and tidy: there should not be any food, coffee cups, papers, and the like left on the table from the previous meeting. Next, set up any equipment you will need for the meeting. If you have a presentation prepared, connect your computer to the projector and ensure it is working before everyone else arrives. You do not want to waste precious meeting time fiddling with technology. If the previous meeting attendees have left their notes on the white board or flipchart, wipe the board down and remove the old paper, providing yourself with a clean slate to begin your meeting.

These preparatory steps will help ensure you can start your meeting on time. Never make the people you have invited to a meeting wait for you; you should always be prepared and ready to begin before everyone else.

Commence your meeting by introducing any newcomers to the group, so everyone at the meeting knows everyone else. Stating the individual's name and his or her role in the project should suffice. Then, draw everyone's attention to the agenda and any action items that must be taken care of during the course of the meeting. Organize the remainder of the meeting around the agenda in order to ensure everything that needs to be taken care of gets covered. As the host of the meeting, it is your responsibility to ensure that participants do not drone on or persistently wander off topic; if this happens, you must intervene and get the discussion back on topic. Sticking to the plan you have laid out will also ensure your meeting finishes on time, so attendees can return to their work or get to their other appointments as needed. If your meeting goes on much longer than planned, chances are at least some participants will have no choice but to leave early in order to accommodate the other items on their schedule for the day.

As decisions are made throughout the meeting, convert them into actions by assigning responsibilities and deadlines. A good strategy to ensure this happens is to jot down things that need to be done or followed up on while the meeting progresses, and spend a few minutes at the end of the meeting going through this list and assigning each item to someone. Circulate this "To Do" list when you get back to your desk after the meeting, so everyone has a copy.

HOW TO DELIVER A SPEECH

Another scenario in which you might find yourself at the front of a room is if you are asked to deliver a speech. Many of the same rules apply in this setting as do when you are running a meeting, such as showing up on time and dressing the part. However, there are a few particular things to note about delivering a speech on a podium, or with a microphone.

First, before you leave home, be sure to choose your outfit carefully. Not only do you want to follow the rules laid out in Chapter 1 to ensure you look professional and confident; you also want to make sure your clothes won't interfere with your speech. Jewellery is notorious for making sounds that carry through microphones and out to your audience, so avoid large bracelets, rings, and necklaces that dangle precariously; these are likely to come into contact with your microphone as you adjust it on the podium or carry it in your hand.

Second, arriving early is crucial, since you want to be able to assess the space in which you will be delivering your speech. If you are able, stand on the podium and test the microphone before everyone arrives. Check to ensure the podium is positioned at an appropriate height for you – you do not want to force your audience to guess who is speaking! Make sure you will be able to see the people you will be speaking to. If the podium is too low, adjust it, or see if there is a stool you may stand on to raise you higher over its edge. Simultaneously, remember that you will want the microphone to be roughly 12 inches from your mouth as you deliver your speech; take care to adjust your podium and the microphone stand accordingly.

By arriving early, you will also get advance notice if there is no podium at all. If this is the case, you will need to prepare to use a handheld microphone. The rules for speaking into a microphone secured to a podium and one that is hand-held are the same, but knowing which you will be using in advance will help to alleviate some of your pre-speech jitters.

Most of our butterflies, jitters and stage-fright are really nothing more than an excess of energy. Some nervousness can be to your advantage as a public speaker. To get your nervous energy working for you rather than against you, keep in mind the following tips:

1. Know your material.
2. Practice!
3. Remember nobody knows what you are going to say.
4. Don't focus on being nervous. Relax and enjoy the moment!

If others have been speaking before you, take the time to readjust the microphone and podium when it is your turn to stand behind it. Be particularly careful to ensure the microphone is secured to the podium, especially if the person using it before you was holding it by hand. You do not want your microphone to slide away in the middle of your speech! If you are the first to speak, make sure the microphone is actually turned on before you begin.

While speaking, remember to pay attention to your body language and think about the message your facial expressions are sending to your audience members. You want to project calm confidence throughout your speech, so stand tall with your feet together, your shoulders gently pulled back and down, and your chin level. Some easy ways to appear nervous include staring down at your podium, shifting your weight from one foot to the other, rapping your knuckles or otherwise tapping the podium impatiently, shuffling the papers your speech is written on, or clutching onto your podium until you have white knuckles. Avoid all of these behaviours, especially because some of them – including paper shuffling and knuckle rapping – will carry through the microphone loudly, muffling your voice and taking away from your speech. Instead, look out at your audience and try to make eye contact so you can connect with them while you speak. As you do this, remember to smile – you do not want to intimidatingly stare down your audience members.

Lastly, make yourself sound calm and collected by speaking at a reasonably slow pace. You want to make sure everyone can hear the important things you have to say and really follow your speech – so do not race through it in seconds! For the same reasons, remember to keep adequate distance (as mentioned above, about twelve inches) from your microphone: never allow your lips to come into contact with it.

VISITING AN OFFICE

In many organizations, the people who have their own offices are the ones with power and influence. That means you want to be particularly conscious of your behaviour in these spaces, in order to gain the favour of those who will likely play some role in your professional advancement.

Casually dropping by someone's office is acceptable only if he or she has asked you to do so. If there is something *you* need to discuss, make an appointment before visiting someone's office. They will almost certainly be busy or in another meeting when you stop by, so making an appointment in advance saves you both time and energy.

Arrive on time for your appointment, and knock before you open the door. If the door is ajar, you should still knock on it a few times to get the person's attention and ask if it is okay for you to enter, rather than just waltzing in. Never barge into someone's office without warning: this is a private space that someone is working in, so you want to avoid disrupting his or her focus, or interrupting another phone call or meeting.

If the person you are meeting with *is* engaged in another phone call or meeting when you arrive, do not eavesdrop. Wait patiently outside, far enough away from the door so that it does not appear you are listening in. Sometimes, people will have chairs outside their office doors that you may sit in while waiting. Your colleague will come get you once the conversation is over, or you may knock on the door once it becomes clear he or she is no longer on the phone.

Do not bring food or drink into someone else's office. Others may have allergies or sensitivities, or be disinclined to certain smells, and you always want to be putting the people around you at ease, not making them uncomfortable.

You also want to devote your undivided attention to your meeting, so do not try to multitask by eating lunch at the same time. The exception to this rule is if you have been asked to provide food or drinks for the meeting; then, you must of course bring what has been requested with you.

Remember that you are in the space that your colleague has to work in for the rest of the day – be respectful! Do not immediately sit down wherever you feel like it; wait to be invited to sit. Never put your feet up or otherwise "lounge" around like you are at home. Also avoid touching things like books, knick-knacks, and any other decorative items in the office without asking first.

Finally, do not over-stay your welcome. You are entering the office to conduct business, so you should leave once the agenda has been attended to. Lingering may annoy the other person, as he or she cannot return to work until you have left. Typically, the person you are meeting with will make it clear that the meeting is over by saying something like, "Do you have any more questions?" or "Thanks for meeting with me." Ask any final questions you might have, then be sure to thank the person for his or her time before leaving the office. If the meeting was with someone you work with every day, there is no need to shake hands. If, however, you met with a client, contact, or business partner you do not see in person regularly, you may shake hands before leaving.

MAKING AND TAKING TELEPHONE CALLS

Think of the many times you have called a customer service line with a question or request for help. The demeanour and professionalism of the person answering the phone and walking you through your problem can either make or break your perception of the entire company. That is why it is equally important for you to exercise impeccable telephone manners at work: you want your colleagues, superiors, and clients to associate you with positive experiences and overall helpfulness.

When receiving an incoming call, pick up the phone within a maximum of three rings. This creates the impression that you are attentive, whereas if you answer after, say, six rings, the person calling will wonder what else you were doing at your desk that whole time before finally deciding you should answer your ringing phone.

Answer the phone with a welcoming greeting, and state your name and your organization's name. For example, you might say something like, "Good morning, this is [your name] from [your organization] speaking." Stating who you are confirms for the person calling that they have in fact reached the correct desk; if you just pick up the phone and say, "Hello?" he or she will have to ask, "Is this the correct number for _____?" In short, make it easy for the person who is attempting to get in touch with you.

After picking up the phone, stop whatever you were working on before. Research shows that multi-tasking is impossible: trying to do two things at once is really just an exercise in switching your focus from one to the other very quickly. Such supposed multi-tasking leads you to perform poorly at both tasks, including your phone conversation. The person calling will likely be able to tell that you are not paying attention, and you will probably miss important details of what he or she is saying, including directions, requests, or new assignments. If you must put someone on speakerphone – say, if you are going to take notes on your conversation – always let him or her know.

While on the phone, stay upbeat and positive. Treat a phone call just as you would an in-person meeting: pretend that you are speaking with the caller face-to-face, and that he or she can see you. This is because our voices carry emotion too; you can "hear" a warm smile and helpful attitude through the phone, just as you can "hear" annoyance and tiredness. It is therefore always a good idea to *actually* smile while you are speaking on the phone, even though no one can see you, because that positive emotion will translate to your listener.

Be sure to speak slowly and clearly into the receiver, so that the caller can hear you well. Focus on enunciating and articulating your words clearly. Do not mutter or mumble, and do not turn your face away from the phone as you are speaking. The one exception to this rule is if you must sneeze or cough; never do this into the receiver. Instead, turn your face away from the phone and even cover the receiver so that the caller does not hear you. Likewise, never belch, blow your nose, snort, eat, drink, or chew gum while on the phone; save these actions for when the phone call is over. If you use a wireless phone for work calls, never answer it in the bathroom.

During your discussion, it is important to be patient and accommodating. Let the caller finish his or her sentences – do not interrupt and start speaking over top of him or her. Remember that listening is the key to conversing effectively; be sure to actually hear, absorb, and process what the caller is saying, especially if he or she is asking you to do something.

If you receive notification of another incoming call during your discussion, simply ignore it and let it go to voicemail. Never put your original caller on hold to take another call. Remember that it is important to respect everyone's time at work; by putting someone on hold, you are forcing him or her to wait around for you to speak with someone else. Finish the first conversation first, then call the second caller back afterward.

Finally, wrap up your phone conversation just as you would a meeting: do not linger, ask unnecessary questions, or begin discussing your personal life. Once you believe the person has the information he or she requires, you may ask, "Is there anything else I can help you with?" Once he or she says "no," use a polite and friendly greeting to sign off, such as "Thanks for calling, and enjoy the rest of your day." Wait for your caller to respond, and then you may both hang up.

Many of the same rules apply when you make a phone call (as opposed to receiving one). Just as you would when answering the phone, say a greeting, your name, and your company name when the person you are calling picks up. For example, you might say, "Good afternoon, this is [your name] calling from [your company's name]." Do not assume that the person you are calling knows it is you; he or she might receive dozens of phone calls daily, so make it easy and simple. The exception to this rule is if you are calling a colleague within your office; if you both work for the same company, there is no need to state your company's name. Instead, you can just say your greeting and your name. If you work for a particularly large company and there is a chance a colleague will not be able to place you, you can also mention your department. For example, you might say, "Good afternoon, this is [your name] calling from [the IT department]."

Be prepared with some idea of what you are going to say to initiate the conversation. Likely, the person you are calling will respond to your initial greeting by saying something like, "Hi [your name], what can I do for you?" Think through what you are going to say to or ask of the person you are calling before actually making the call. This is another opportunity to demonstrate your respect for your colleagues' and clients' time: you do not want to have to pause and think about the purpose for your call while on the phone.

Just as you would when answering the phone, stay upbeat and positive throughout your conversation. Articulate your words clearly and speak slowly so you can be heard and understood. Do not multitask, and do not take other incoming calls. This will be interpreted as particularly rude if you were the one to initiate the call; the person will wonder why you initiated contact if you were just going to continue doing other things anyway.

When you have addressed the purpose of your call, be sure to wrap up the conversation in a timely manner. Remember that you are potentially taking the person away from his or her other work, so do not ask more questions than necessary or delve into personal issues that have nothing to do with work. Always thank the person for his or her time before you sign off. Your concluding exchange might go something like:

> *You:* "Thanks very much for taking the time to answer my questions."
> *The person you called:* "Of course!"
> *You:* "Enjoy the rest of your day."
> *The person you called:* "You too."

Then you may both hang up.

Often, the person you are calling will be unable to answer the phone, and your call will go to voicemail. Every single time you make a call, you should be prepared for this to happen. That is because awkward, disorganized, rambling voicemails are excruciating to listen to and will annoy the person you are calling. So, whenever you make a call, take a moment before you dial to think through what you would say in a voicemail. Planning in advance will help you avoid saying "um" and "uh" a lot during your message, both of which sound unprofessional and as though you are disorganized. Conversely, when making a call that you believe will go to voicemail, you should also be prepared for the possibility that the person might actually answer the phone.

When leaving a message, introduce yourself just as you would if you were speaking directly to the person. Never say, "Guess who this is!" Not only is this overly casual and unprofessional; it will also waste the person's time, as they may genuinely not know who is calling.

Begin your message by addressing the person you are calling by name, and, just as with an active phone call, letting he or she know who is calling. You might say something like, "Good afternoon [person's name], this is [your name] from [your company.]" Stating the other person's name ensures your message gets to the right person.

Make sure your message contains all the information necessary, without being overly long or rambling. The points you must include are your name, company, the nature of the business you need to attend to, and your contact information so the person can follow up with you. You may wish to repeat your phone number, stating it twice, so that the person has time to write it down and double check that it is correct without having to listen to your entire message over again. You never ever want to leave a message so long that the machine cuts you off. Keep it brief and to the point, while still conveying the details necessary.

It is particularly important to speak clearly over a message, as you have no one active on the receiving end to indicate whether or not you are audible. So take your time and articulate your words precisely. You want to make sure the person you are leaving a message for can make out your name and contact information – otherwise, you will not be receiving a call back!

Wrap up your message gracefully and on a positive note

by saying something like, "Thank you for your time, and I look forward to hearing back from you." So, your phone message might follow a structure something like this:

"Good afternoon [person's name], this is [your name] calling from [your organization]. I would like to discuss [state the purpose of your call concisely] with you at your earliest convenience. Please return my call when you have a moment. You can reach me at [provide your phone number]. Once again, that's [repeat your phone number]. Thank you for your time, and I look forward to hearing back from you."

EMAIL ETIQUETTE

Email has become the preferred method of professional communication since it is quicker, easier, and more affordable than phone calls. But as more of us come to see emails in a similar light to texts or instant messages, the greater the risk we run of being overly casual, sloppy, and even unintentionally offensive in our digital correspondence.

Any email you send from your official work address projects an image representative of your company. The address bears your organization's name, so you want the recipient to associate that organization with professionalism, clarity, and efficiency – not sloppiness or carelessness. To that end, you should always do the following when sending work-related emails:

1. Start with a salutation. Never jump right into the body of an email without addressing your recipient. You might begin by writing something like, "Hi [name of recipient]" or "Good morning [name of recipient]." After this initial salutation, skip a line, and then begin your message. Do not use "Dear."

2. Include a subject line. Make it easy for the person you are emailing to get a sense of what your longer message is going to be about. A blank subject line can make it seem like you rushed through composing your email, and did not bother taking the time to write these few simple words out. Good subject lines consist of a few words at most and give your recipient advanced notice of what you are going to say in the body of the email. Do not, however, write the entire question or statement you intend to email someone about in the subject line – that is what the email message is for!

3. *Keep it professional.* Just as you want to avoid spewing all the details of your personal life over the phone, avoid writing an essay about your weekend or upcoming vacation in an email. Similarly, do not ask prying questions about your recipient's private life. Politely get to the point, and let the person you are emailing know the purpose of your message right away. Also maintain a professional tone by writing in a simple, legible font (such as Times New Roman), black type (rather than bright, difficult-to-read colours), and using proper capitalization. Never use ALL CAPS, as most people interpret this as though you are shouting at them; it comes across as rude and aggressive. For the same reasons, never curse in an email, nor participate in forwarding chain letters to people in your office. The general rule of thumb is that you should never write something in an email that you would not want to see published in the newspaper.

4. *Be brief.* Avoiding personal chitchat will also help keep your email short and to the point. Remember, you always want to respect the other work your colleagues, business partners, and clients have vying for their time, so state what it is you are emailing them about concisely, in as few sentences as possible.

5. *Sign off.* Just as you would a telephone call, wrap up your email with a polite concluding line. For example, you might write, "Thank you for your time, and I look forward to hearing from you." Especially if you are emailing a superior, business partner, or client, you do not want to appear harsh or rude by stating what you need without any pleasantries to soften your request. After your brief, polite sign-off, you may opt for an email signature instead of simply typing your name. Make sure your signature contains all the necessary information your recipient would likely need, including your job title and telephone number, and double check to make sure all of that information is correct. You do not want to inconvenience anyone by having them call a phone number listed in your signature that is not actually yours.

6. *Spellcheck.* Never send an email without proofreading it

first. Sometimes, a sentence will sound good in your head as you are writing it out, but may come off as awkward or confusing. Re-reading your message will give you a chance to make sure you are saying what you actually meant to say in as clear a manner as possible. It will also give you the chance to catch any embarrassing spelling and grammar mistakes that would otherwise make your message look sloppy and rushed.

7. Send to the right people. Before you click "Send," double-check the list of recipients you have included. If your message contains sensitive or confidential information, you must take extra care to ensure it does not end up in the wrong person's inbox. Conversely, make sure you have included everyone who needs to hear the information you are writing about; make a conscious effort to remember everyone who is involved in a given project and include them on all related communications so they have the opportunity to know what is expected of them.

Once you have sent your email, give the recipient adequate time to respond. If you have chosen to communicate with someone in this manner, do not immediately try to contact them another way, such as by phone. Calling and emailing someone at the same time – unless it is extremely urgent – will seem desperate and anxious, suggesting to the recipient that you struggle to remain calm under pressure.

When responding to emails, rather than initiating contact through them, all of the same rules apply. However, you should also be conscious of the time it takes you to respond. People are often hoping for and expecting a fairly rapid response to an email; always get back to them within 24 to 48 hours. If you will be away from the office on vacation, due to illness, or for personal reasons and will be unable to check your emails, set up your account to deploy an automatic "Out Of Office" response to everyone who attempts to contact you within that period of time. Include in your autoreply the name and contact information for one of your colleagues who will be able to address the matters typically expected of you (and do not forget to ask that colleague for assistance before including him or her in your autoreply). This allows the people trying to reach you to make alternative arrangements, rather than waiting for a reply they will not receive. Do not forget to switch your autoreply off once you return.

TEXTING TIPS

Texting (in a professional context) should be reserved for situations requiring a quick response time and where a casual tone and approach are acceptable. Here are some tips.

1. Reply promptly, within five minutes of receiving the text if possible. Texts are convenient if you are running late. Include the estimated time of arrival.
2. Don't text at inappropriate times – for example, in movie theatres, funerals, or meetings (or, of course, while driving).
3. Keep it short! Texting is meant for brief messages.
4. Don't text sensitive news (e.g., breaking up with your partner, death, or a serious illness).
5. Always re-read your texts before sending them. It takes only two seconds to proofread.
6. Don't send too many attachments.
7. Double-check the recipient of your texts.
8. Use proper grammar.
9. Avoid using too many emojis.
10. Don't text too early or late in the day.
11. Don't text while eating or drinking with others. Excuse yourself if an emergency arises.
12. Do not text while another person is speaking, unless it is extremely important to do so. If you must text, offer a brief explanation immediately so you won't hurt the speaker's feelings. Consider excusing yourself if you don't want to share private details.
13. Texting a thank-you note is not okay. You should always call, send a physical card, or send an e-card.
14. Don't text while driving – ever!
15. Don't text while walking. Step to the side, out of harm's (and other people's) way. Do not block the passage.
16. Don't forget to sign off with your name.

CUSTOMER SERVICE SKILLS

Whether you work in entry-level retail or as the CEO of a

Always send your client off while smiling, so their last memory of you will be a positive one. Say something polite, such as "Thank you for stopping by," to conclude your interaction. Leaving your clients on an upbeat, happy note will solidify their positive perception of you and the company you are representing.

massive corporation, you will be required to provide services to your customers or clients at times. Just as your demeanor over the telephone will impact your clients' perception of your company, so too will your ability to politely provide useful information face-to-face.

Always maintain a positive, helpful attitude when interacting with your clients. Greet each one with a warm smile and salutation. You might say, for example, "Good morning," "Good afternoon," or "Good evening." You may do so when moving through settings where your clients are likely to be, such as if you are walking through the halls and waiting room in your office. You should do the same if you are providing customer service and assisting clients more directly; if you are expected to direct clients to a particular location, for example, you may want to add a question to your initial greeting, so the clients know you are the one they can turn to for help. For example, you might say, "Good morning, how may I help you?" just as you would if someone called you on the phone.

After greeting your customer, pay close attention to what he or she is saying. Never assume you know what a customer needs. Remember from Chapter 2 that people appreciate feeling as though they are being listened to; your customers will view you and your company more positively if they feel their needs have been heard and addressed. To that end, always be sensitive and sympathetic to whatever your client has to say: do not dismiss his or her concerns, and do your best to be helpful. If you do not know how to address a particular question or concern, you are also being helpful if you direct the client to the individual who *will* know what to do. Never leave a client with questions and no advice regarding how they might find answers.

If you must bring a customer to another employee in order to address his or her concerns, always accompany him or her, rather than abandoning the client to wander off in search of the other employee. If you are unable to leave your post, provide the most clear, detailed directions possible. Instead of pointing, gesture with an open hand. Make sure the customer understands where to go before moving on to your next client.

Conclusion

Throughout this book, you have learned the many settings and interactions in which a strong grasp of etiquette can only benefit you. While many – especially younger – people today dismiss these practices, thinking of them as nothing more than frivolous table manners, the reality is that the entire employment market is saturated with the expectation that employees will be courteous, professional, and refined during interviews, business meetings, networking events, and at the office every single day. If you hope one day be counted as an employee of any organization, you must live up to these expectations, and even surpass them if you dream of attaining a promotion or raise in our increasingly competitive work environment.

While it might seem intimidating at first, etiquette is in fact very straightforward. As you embark upon your first job interview, attend a networking event, or prepare to dine with a promising business partner, you must simply remember that etiquette is *really* about making others feel comfortable in your presence. By dressing, speaking, eating, and communicating in the ways we have discussed, you will quickly become a master at making people feel at ease.

Acknowledgements

I would like to express gratitude to Prof. Peter Harris and Maureen Harris for encouraging me to write this book.

I would like to thank Prof. Lorne Tepperman for introducing me to Nicole Meredith.

This book would not have happened without Nicole's support and creative writing skills.

A special thank you to my publisher David Stover for all of his support.

Index of Key Topics and Tips

The most important topics and tips covered in the book are listed in the following index for ease of reference.

Attire, 4–7
Body adornments, 8–9
Body language, 21–22
Business cards, 27–29
Conversation tips, 24–26
Dining, 31ff.
  Basic tips, 32–34
  Bread and dinner rolls, 40–41
  Checklist, 49
  Chopsticks, 50–51
  Coffee, 48
  Dessert, 48
  Dining in host's home, 53–55
  Dining out, 52–53
  Glassware, 36, 38–39
  Main course, 46, 48
  Place settings, 34–39
  Salad, 44–45
  Soup, 42–44
  Toasts, 39–40
  Utensils, 36, 45–47, 50–51
  Wine glass, 34
Email etiquette, 73–76
Entering a room, 14–15
Hair, 9
Handshakes, 15–18
Hygiene, 8
Introductions, 18–20
Make-up, 9–10
Meetings, 60–65
Name badges, 20–21
Pre-interview checklists, 11–13
Public speaking, 65–67
Scent, 7–8
Telephone etiquette, 68–73
Texting etiquette, 76–78
Thank-you notes, 29–30
Visiting an office, 67–68
Working a room, 22–24

Endorsements and Thank You's

Over the years, I have received many words of thanks and a considerable amount of feedback from those who have enrolled in my etiquette classes. Although the focus in this book is on the benefits of mastering basic etiquette for those finishing their education and entering the workforce for the first time, brushing up on etiquette can benefit students still in school as people who have been out working for some time.

After teaching a group of international students at a Toronto-area college, I received the following lovely email:

> *I wish I could thank you enough for the information you shared with the students of Seneca College today. I learned a lot from today's lesson, and feel a lot more confident and motivated for my upcoming interviews.*
>
> *Thanks a lot for the lunch and the warm hospitality of the Faculty Club. It was great meeting such a nice person like you and I hope to see you again in the future.*

Here is a selection of other comments from students:

> *Thank you so much for this past week's dining etiquette seminar. Your lessons were easy to remember, simple to follow and delightful to learn. I only wish more of my friends were able to attend!*
>
> *I will endeavour to put these skills into practice as soon and as often as I can.*

> *I'm a student who truly benefited from your training. I just wanted to say thank you for the etiquette session yesterday. It was such perfect timing since I immediately attended two info sessions the day after, and for the first time ever, two recruiters actively asked for my information, so I'd like to think your training played a big role!*

> *Coming from Middle East, I was blessed enough to be able to emigrate to Canada. I have had the chance to dine*

in the finest hotels in Dubai, but in the session today I learned a lot, thanks to your perseverance and excellence in what you do....

My daughter is just six years old. We may wait for another year or two to attend a session with her, in order to make the most out of it.

I am a student at the University of Waterloo.
Thank you for running an amazing etiquette dinner session as part of the What's Next conference yesterday.
I can now say that I know how to eat with confidence in a formal setting (well, I will, after 21 days of practice!).

Thank you for hosting and leading a wonderful etiquette lunch at the Faculty Club yesterday. I learned many new things to be aware of when dining and attending cocktail receptions. All the tips will be helpful throughout my career.

We attendees of tonight's Etiquette Club formal dinner are very appreciative of your lesson today. You spent almost three hours teaching us how to dine properly but without eating any food yourself! I hope you had something to eat prior to the event.

I was my honour to participate and I sincerely wish to see you again in future events. The lesson is extremely useful and I learned a lot from you tonight.

Another huge success! On behalf of the etiquette club, I would like to express my gratitude for a great session and hope to make this event a staple for every year.
I have heard feedback from several of our members and their consensus was that the event was well organized, the venue was beautiful, the food was delicious (best apple crumble they ever had!), and, most importantly, that they had learned so much. One alumna also wished that she had taken this course sooner and said that she will utilize her skills for future business settings.
Last year I expressed the desire to work with you at the Club. I cannot believe how much I've grown since then.

The experience has been a dream come true!

I've also been delighted to teach etiquette at the Dovercourt Boys and Girls Club. You're never too young to learn good manners. Many thanks to the director Sheldon Taylor, Mattéo Severino, and all the staff and boys and girls for their support and love. Below is a picture taken at the club, with a "Please and Thank You" banner that the students made.

About the Author

Leanne Pepper has served as the general manager of the Faculty Club at the University of Toronto since 1994. Prior to that, she was general manager of McMaster University's Faculty Club. She is a certified etiquette and protocol consultant and image coach, having graduated from the Protocol School of Washington, and she is also a graduate of the respected George Brown College program in hospitality and culinary arts. A native of London, Ont., she says that helping people, both through her work in the hospitality industry and as an etiquette consultant and coach, has always been her passion. In what spare time Leanne has, she enjoys traveling, cycling, gardening, birdwatching, and creating new dishes in her home kitchen. Her favourite quotation is this advice from Maya Angelou: "I've learned that people will forget what you said, people will forget what you did, but people will never forget how you made them feel."